Sexy and SPARKLING after 40

Gail –
Believe in Your
Sparkling Magnificence!

Love,
Shari

Praise For Sexy and Sparkling After 40

"Sherri Nickols has written a sexy, sassy book that will inspire you to turn up your light and step up your game. A delightful read . . . juicy and joyful!"

~ Katherine Woodward Thomas
Author of Calling in "The One" and co-founder of the Feminine Power Global Community

"With wit, wisdom and enthusiasm, *Sexy and Sparkling After 40* provides solutions for all women who have forgotten how to access their feminine, playful side. Don't miss the end of the book's 'Romance-Capades,' they are priceless!"

~ Arielle Ford, author The Soulmate Secret

"Before any woman can find a long-lasting love relationship, she first needs to deepen her relationship with herself. Sherri Nickols' 7-step SPARKLE System will guide you to the radiant person within. Through her candid and honest self-portrayal, she leads you through your own journey of self-discovery. With humor and humility, Sherri shows you the way to re-connect with your sparkle."

~Dr. Diana Kirschner
Bestselling author of Love in 90 Days: The Essential Guide to Finding Your Own True Love & Sealing the Deal: The Love Mentor's Guide to Lasting Love

"For all the women out there who have lost their sparkle, this is your wake-up call and your permission slip to bust out of your slump, slip on those stilettos, and rediscover YOU!"

~Lisa Steadman
Best selling author, It's A Breakup, Not A Breakdown

"Daily life and competing roles can take their toll on a woman's 'sparkle.' Its a challenge to keep your love of life, and self, from gathering dust on a back shelf. But take heart, Sherri Nickols gives us the tools to reconnect with the radiance and luster that were there all along. This warmly and wisely written book is like a comforting, supportive chat with a best friend. The seven steps outlined by Sherri provide a wonderful road map back to our sparkling essential selves, and make for an exciting, thoroughly enjoyable journey of confidence and self-discovery."

~Deborah Vance-Maher, working mom

"When it comes to explaining why the sparkle leaves modern marriages, Sherri has her finger on the pulse of one very important piece: the diminishing and devaluation of the feminine spirit. In our ever-evolving modern culture, it's become commonplace for women to take on the masculine 'get it done' energy that works so well for men. As Sherri shares in her own personal story, this path fails women time and again because it dims the light that makes up the true feminine spirit. Sherri expertly shows women how to reignite her feminine energy and connect with her true 'inner sparkle' to create the life and love she's yearning for. For any woman searching for 'what's missing' in her life, this book is a must read to ensure that you're truly connected to your most loving, vibrant feminine self."

~Melanie Gorman
Sr. VP YourTango Experts

"It is up to each of us to create our own destiny. Manifesting the life we desire begins with understanding who we are, what we're passionate about, and then living authentically from that place. Sherri Nickols has discovered a unique way to help women journey through that path of self-discovery. Sherri has walked the path she lays out before you. With honesty, humor and courageous self-disclosure, she guides you through her step-by-step process so that you never have to feel alone or unsupported. Sherri shows you that living the life of your dreams begins with a heroine's inward journey towards finding and reclaiming your power."

~Patrick Snow
International Best-Selling author of Creating Your Own Destiny and The Affluent Entrepreneur

"If you've ever felt like a diamond in the rough, Sherri Nickols 7-step system will help you re-discover your sparkling essence and fall in love with yourself. With real examples, lots of love, and practical guidance—you'll feel supported as you journey to discover your multi-faceted self like never before. By the time you've finished her book, you'll have the courage, creativity and confidence to live your most brilliant life."

~Christine Kloser, "The Transformation Catalyst"
Founder of TransformationalAuthor.com

"With all the hustle and bustle of daily life, I'd lost my sparkle and forgotten how to play and have fun. After working with Sherri, reading her book, and applying her techniques and strategies, I found my sensual playful spirit again. You know that old saying, 'if mama ain't happy then nobody's happy'? Well, *thanks to Sherri and this system, everybody around here is veerrrryyyy happy!"*

~Karyn Collins, Owner
Quantum Photo Design

"Sherri Nickols understands the importance of women discovering their own sensuality and connecting with their feminine energy. Both are essential elements to becoming an attractive and approachable woman. Through honest self-disclosure and her step-by-step process,

Sherri shows women how to find their way back to their vibrant, glowing selves so that others will be drawn to them like a moth to flame."

~Patty Contenta
www.sensualitysecrets.com

"A powerful formula for reinventing your love life! Sherri Nickols unlocks what every man over forty is looking for in a woman. This book gives you the step-by-step process for renewing your radiance and attracting the love you want."

~Mat Boggs
Best-Selling Co-Author of "Project Everlasting"
Creator of Cracking The Man Code

"The perfect book for any woman experiencing a life-altering relationship change. It lifted me to new heights of encouragement and strength. Sherri's writing is very entertaining and unique, enticing you with the desire for the next tidbit of information and guidance she has to offer. A definite must have for your reading and self-help collection."

~Dr. Lana Bettencourt

"If you are a woman who has too much on her plate and has lost her luster for life, have no fear, Sherri Nickols is here. In her funny, down-to-earth, delightful book, "Sexy and Sparkling after 40," Sherri shows you how to reconnect with your feminine power so you can rock the world and live that exciting, romantic life you have been yearning for!"

~Kimberly Riggins author of Love Your Naked Ass

"Sexy and SPARKLING after 40" provides in my opinion the ultimate road map for women over 40 who want to bring happiness and joy back into their lives. Women who read and follow Sherri's advice will enjoy a fun-filled personal journey of regaining their feminine essence, energizing their playful spirit while becoming a magnet for attracting adventure and romance.

~ *Earl Bell author of Winning in Baseball and Business*

"Sherri Nickols captures exactly how it feels to have lost that zest or sparkle for life and how to re-ignite it with ease. She powerfully embraces the ups and downs in life and love, while tenderly showing the steps to remain vibrant, luscious, delighted, relaxed and playful. It's written in a way that respects the intelligent business woman and youthful innocent girl within each of us.

This is a MUST READ for ALL WOMEN ... Embracing your feminine self in all its' glory is lovely, powerful, and brings an inner peace like no other. We were created to be radiant creatures and Sherri lovingly reminds us of the beauty in that!"

~ *Stephanie Sterling, Business Woman*

"Real life can pound away at your sense of beauty. Once you hit 40, it can feel like you are only going through the motions where romance is concerned.

Much more than just a dating book, Sexy and Sparkling is a great read for any woman over 40 who wants to feel more passion, joy and happiness. Full of spiritual insights, humor, and how to tips to conquer the 13 relationship culprits which rob you of your sparkle, this book will make you laugh and maybe even blush a bit. Be sure to try the 15 Romance Adventures at the back of the book- fun activities to get his attention and create some lasting memories together.

If you've ever wanted a romance talk with a girlfriend a la Sex and the City, this book is for you!

~ *Lynne B. Klippel "Book Strategist and Publisher"*

7 **STEPS** to Revitalize Your Radiance &
Create Romantic Adventure in Your Life!

Sherri Nickols

New York

Sexy and Sparkling After 40: 7 Steps to Revitalize Your Radiance & Create Romantic Adventure in Your Life!

Printed in the United States of America

Published in the United States by
Aviva Publishing
Lake Placid, NY
518-523-1320
www.avivapubs.com

Address all inquiries to:

11693 San Vicente Blvd. #304
Los Angeles, CA 90049
www.sexyandsparkling.com
Sherri@sexyandsparkling.com

Includes bibliographical references

LCCN: 2011937470
ISBN # - 978-1-935586-44-9

Cover design: Dotti Albertine
Editing: Elizabeth Wolf
Author Photograph: Corey Nickols
Book layout and design: Andrew Little

Author's Note:
The stories in this book are mostly actual with a few composites but the names have been changed to protect the individuals' privacy.

This book is dedicated to my beautiful, sweet mom who filled my life with light and joy, and taught me how to love.
I miss you mom - with all my heart.

Acknowledgements

The journey of writing this book has been an illuminating experience full of twists and turns. I could not have done it without the love, cheering, guidance and generous support of so many amazing people. It took a village to get liftoff and I am deeply grateful to everyone who helped make this book a reality.

First and foremost to my insightful friend Moshe Aelyon and my caring brother Greg who gave me the courage and motivation to finally put pen to paper. After 10 years of talking about it, you both inspired me to do it. Those fateful conversations were definitely divine appointments.

Huge thanks to my amazing, big-hearted angels Marisa and Brett Grimes, Carrie and Craig Konjoyan, Brenda and Steve Tamkin, Maureen and Ed Castro, and Robert Andelson and Alex LaPiana for believing in me. I am blessed to have such incredible lifelong friends who have always stood by me. Without your generous contributions and support this book would not be in print.

A very heartfelt thank you to my dear friends Vicki and Drew Dusebout for opening your beautiful home to me for months on end. Your generosity afforded me a magical and tranquil haven of inspiration to write this book. Thank you for providing such a comfy, cozy, safe space for me to create. I am so grateful for your lifelong love and support of my endeavors.

Big thanks to my cherished friend Patti Smith for being a key part of the brainstorming and marketing, for your endless encouragement and cheerleading when it all felt impossible, for your unwavering enthusiasm and support of my message, for believing in me when I didn't believe in myself.

To my incredibly talented and creative friends: Jon Condell, huge thanks for your insightful suggestions to the manuscript, for your truth-telling and tough love when I needed it, for your ability to see the big picture, for your constant love and support and...for the never-ending laughter. Special thanks to Alberto Mendoza for your belief in this project and your sizzling Romance-Capade contributions – love your mischievous mind! Greatly appreciate your friendship and support. A big splashy thanks to Chris Mahdesian and Christopher Carnino for your brilliant vision and clever contributions, for your caring support and outrageous humor. Deep appreciation to Lori Ann Robinson for your creative costume contributions, designing mind, imagination, artistic sense and loyal friendship.

I am grateful to my wonderful circle of friends for their ongoing love and support. There are so many of you and at the risk of missing some, I thank: Nina for your uplifting words of encouragement and positive spirit; Joe and Alicia for providing me with a warm and safe place to land when writing and working my process, and for delightful home-cooked meals and your caring hearts; Janka for your soul sister support, wise and inspiring pep talks, consistent love and faith in me, and tons of laughter; Ann for asking me the hard questions when I needed it the most and loving me through them; Sue, my friend and mastermind partner, for your wisdom, enthusiasm, urging when needed and referral to Elizabeth; Judy for your cheerleading and encouragement; Deb for your spiritual wisdom and contribution to the book and for reminding me what's important; Jane Mnoian for your intuitiveness and gentle push to write this book; Karen for your excitement and enthusiasm.

Big thanks to Dotti Albertine for designing a beautiful cover that perfectly captures the essence and message of this book; Lynne Klippel and Rick Hill for reading my manuscript and guiding me with much-needed feedback; Patrick Snow for invaluable advice on how to self-publish and market a book; Donna Mazzitelli for helping me with the endorsements; Andrew Little for keen attention to detail and laying out a beautiful book; and Coleen Smith for well executed illustrations.

Special thanks to my editor, Elizabeth Wolf, who skillfully shaped and rearranged the manuscript with her wise and masterful mind. From the moment I spoke with her I loved her energy, enthusiasm and authenticity and knew she totally got my message. She was also instrumental in helping me stay the course to complete this book, keeping me focused when I was overwhelmed and ready to pull my hair out. I appreciate your friendship and professionalism.

To all the actresses and public figures who have touched my life and helped me move forward on my path, especially: Sarah Jessica Parker, Dolly Parton, Jennifer Aniston, Kate Winslet, Cheryl Crow, Heather Locklear, Sandra Bullock, Oprah Winfrey, Maya Angelou, Marilyn Monroe, Reese Witherspoon, Meryl Streep, and Goldie Hawn.

Deep appreciation to my family for their encouragement, love and support of what is, without a doubt, the greatest professional challenge of my career. I'm grateful for your understanding of the long hours, weekend work and myopic focus. I love and appreciate each of you very much. You all have offered advice, suggestions, pep talks, artistic opinion and words of encouragement throughout my journey—this has been invaluable to me and kept my spirits high. Special thanks to my nephews: Riley, your help with endorsements was above and beyond, and Corey, your photographic talent is amazing.

And, of course, deeply heartfelt thanks to my students and clients who shared their dreams, challenges and victories with me. You inspired this book through your courage to overcome obstacles, your perseverance to break free from fears and limiting beliefs, your bravery to go to the gunges of your soul to heal and then create a sparkling new life. You are my teachers. I thank you for enriching this book.

Finally, my deepest gratitude goes to Janet and Philippe Buillet, who led me back to God. He is really the One who made this book possible.

CONTENTS

Prologue: How It All Began 1
Introduction 17

The SPARKLE System™

Chapter 1: Get Your Sparkle On! 27
Chapter 2: Ways We Lose Our Radiance 43
Chapter 3: Soul Sister Support 69
Chapter 4: S...See Your Bright Future 81
Chapter 5: P...Pinpoint Your Passions 95
Chapter 6: A...Adjust Your Attitude 113
Chapter 7: R...Renew Your Relationship With YOU! 117
Chapter 8: K...Know Who You Are 145
Chapter 9: L...Laugh and Play 163
Chapter 10: E...Embrace Your Life 179
Chapter 11: Sexy and Sparkling Forever 193
The Diamond Belief 200

Passport to Passion
The Romance-Capades™

Chapter 12: The Art of the Invitation 207
RC-1: Bring Back the Spark 214

RC-2:	Dream Angel	218
RC-3:	Love Letter	222
RC-4:	Neptune's Desire	226
RC-5:	Island Fever	230
RC-6:	Casino Royal	234
RC-7:	It Takes Two to Tango	238
RC-8:	Let's Get Twisted	242
RC-9:	Meet Me at the Kasbah	246
RC-10:	Let's Burn it Up	250
RC-11:	The Love Lounge	254
RC-12:	Paris at Dawn	258
RC-13:	Pirate's Booty	262
RC-14:	Mystery & Mischief	266
RC-15:	Playboy Mansion	270

Resources 274
About the Author 278
Coaching & Products 280
Share Your Story 283
QR 284

PROLOGUE

How it All Began...

Growing up with a controlling mother who wore the pants in the family made taking the helm in my own marriage seem like the most natural thing in the world to do. Although it worked for my mother, it proved disastrous for me. My well-intentioned heroic actions ended in unhappily ever after as I helplessly watched my husband walk out the door...for good.

After years of trying to "make it work," I had failed. I felt betrayed, shocked, and heartbroken.

Life as I knew it had just ended.

Life as it could be was about to begin.

Here's the story of how this book—and my reinvention—were born.

A River Called Denial

Who knew my husband, Stephano, had an entirely different set of morals than I, thinking it was okay to live a double life with a woman in another state (out of state doesn't count?).

Who knew I had enough tears to fill the Pacific Ocean (*and* the Atlantic).

Who knew my heart could endure such pain and continue to beat? (Hel-LO, *Guinness Book of World Records!*)

Who knew that in trying to fix everything, I would lose it all—most significantly myself.

I guess there were a lot of things I didn't know. Or chose not to know. Regardless, I was so stunned by the sudden ending of my 13-year relationship that I often just stood, frozen, staring into space. That is, until the uncontrollable shaking took over.

On the bright side, it *was* one heck of a diet. Dropping 15 pounds in 10 days permanently changed my metabolic rate, allowing me to kiss my lifelong battle of the bulge goodbye. Woohooo! Finally, a change I could embrace!

It was also the first evidence I had that good really does come from bad. And believe me, a boatload of positives presented in rapid succession, gifting me with my great big *Aha!* moment.

Yes, I got the boot. Big time. There was no denying that. But here's another undeniable truth: when you're not paying attention to all those larger-than-life signs flashing in your face, the powers that be swoop in and take over. It can feel like an ambush, but it's always a rescue. Take my story as an example:

Was I happy in my marriage? Not exactly.

Was I crazy in love with my husband? Not so much.

Were my needs being met? Not really.

Was I sweeping all those glaring, red flags under the carpet?

You bet!

Why? Because at the time it just seemed too messy and inconvenient to deal with the truth. You could say I'd developed an affinity for blinders. I'd chosen to pretend my life was everything I wanted it to be.

In fact, I was dying a *slow death.*

When there are so many disappointments in a marriage it's easy to lose respect for your partner and yourself, go into denial, and push down the obvious to keep everything "looking good."

But have you ever noticed when you're drunk with denial, there comes that inevitable moment when the truth finds you and smacks you sober? This is exactly what happened to me. And as awful as this awakening was, it was truly a blessing in disguise.

The truth was, I was tired of my husband's "promises" that never materialized, tired of his double standards, tired of carrying the financial responsibility, tired of rescuing him, tired of his ego, tired of his selfish bedroom behavior, tired of his traipsing off when I needed him (also known as abandonment), tired of feeling like the man in the marriage, and *really* tired of his Mediterranean temper.

Jeez, with that laundry list I should have kissed the cosmos instead of crying my eyes out when he left me.

Interestingly, after a few months of pity parties I was able to take a nanosecond break from blaming my ex. Guess what happened? A surprising sliver of enlightenment slipped in. I started to see *my* dirty laundry, what MY part was in this life-changing reality.

Whoever said it takes two to tango wasn't lying. My big "Aha" moment sounded more like an "Ugh." To say it wasn't pretty is an understatement. Rather than setting boundaries, standing in my truth, honoring my divine feminine, being honest about my feelings and leaving the relationship when my needs were repeatedly not met, I stepped up to the plate and did a gender switch. Yes indeedy, I became the man. Well, somebody had to, right? (Let's hear it for justifications!)

Mr. Me, Large and in Charge

I suppose now is as good a time as any to let you in on the dirty details of what led me to this macho stance.

Once upon a time, many moons ago, I trekked across Europe to quench my soul's thirst for adventure. Through a series of events, I was introduced to a tall, dark and handsome man in an exotic Mediterranean country. A budding bicontinental romance blossomed, and after a few years Stephano and I took our relationship to the next level. Others thought our marriage was rather unconventional, primarily because it remained bicontinental. I thought it was thrilling—just enough space and plenty of adventure. But truth be told, living apart had its drawbacks—like being in the dark about your partner's daily decisions and their crippling consequences.

You see, one night I got a shocking call from my entrepreneur-husband's best friend, making me feel like the heroine in a Sidney Sheldon novel. Apparently Stephano had made some bad business decisions—so bad he had to be smuggled out of his country in the middle of the night. He faced bankruptcy, mafia madness, and total shame. Since our businesses were connected that meant we *both* had to start over.

The next day Stephano arrived in America. Nothing could have prepared me for the enormity of his damaged ego and broken soul.

Even though he was safely tucked away with me in the States, far from the gangsters who wanted his life, his self-esteem was so low you couldn't have scraped it from the sidewalk.

As he settled into a deep depression I became what I thought our relationship needed—an aggressive breadwinner. I made it my personal mission to save him and "us." After all, we had lots of dreams and none of them included an untimely death or being in debt for the rest of our lives.

Unwittingly I bid farewell to my fun feminine spirit and said hello to Mr. Me. That was the beginning of the end.

Slowly Stephano and I regrouped. He was offered a partnership with friends and I worked as an outside sales rep in the fashion textile industry where the sky was the limit in earning potential. With a goal the size of a glacier I worked like a banshee; little by little we chipped away at his enormous debt. After several years we were almost ready to join the ranks of our friends and amass the American dream—a home and bambinos!

Finally, as the leaves began to turn and autumn was upon us we were about to be debt free. But we were entering yet another holiday season childless, so we decided to step it up to in vitro. Squeamish and unable to even look at a needle, here I was giving myself hormone shots. I begged for bravery and prayed that it would all be worthwhile.

Life was humming along at a full clip with our weekends devoted to house hunting, biking and hanging with friends. All the more we were about to enter into a business deal with one of our favorite couples. At long last, life was good! Even normal.

Then one fateful morning in December my carefully controlled life changed. While Stephano was out getting his national newspaper, I had an inner nudge to enter his home office. Just as I did his phone began to ring.

Expecting his answering machine to pick up without volume, I was surprised to hear a syrupy Southern drawl fill the room. "Hi Sweetie, I found us an apartment and I'm on my way to the doctor." It was at that moment reality hit me—and HARD!

Suddenly, the room became a tilt-a-whirl. I couldn't breathe. I gasped for air and grabbed the phone in the same moment. She hung up as soon as she heard my voice. I asked myself, "How could this be?" I felt like an inflatable doll whose plug just got pulled.

When I discovered my husband had been masquerading as a single man for the majority of our marriage and living a double life with a woman in Chicago for the last several months, my confusion and pain turned to outrage.

Then again, divine intervention is an unexpected gift. No wonder I couldn't get pregnant! God was protecting me from a permanent lifeline to this secretive man I suddenly realized I never knew at all. And although the situation was completely black and white to me, there was still sadness, fear of the future, and intense grieving—not only for the end of my marriage but also for the loss of the woman I gave up so many years ago.

The Truth Sets Us Free

At my very core I knew that once I got through this tunnel of darkness, I would create new dreams. But I wasn't sure how to find my *Self* again.

I knew how to do career. I was quite successful at that. But I had no clue how to do feminine. I needed to balance myself and I desperately wanted to get that fun, adventurous, carefree woman back. But how?

This is where Mr. Me actually came in handy. With take-charge enthusiasm, curiosity, and determination, I embarked on the most important journey of my life—finding my way back to Ms. Me.

Who do you turn to in times like this, with such an important mission at hand? You want honesty, you want direction, and you want it from someone you can trust.

I called in my closest confidants for a frank critique. The most poignant and enlightening insight came from Jon, my lifelong friend. He gifted me with his keen perception and observation to set me on my perfect path.

One night when I was feeding my sadness with a box of See's candy (Mary See can be so comforting!), I asked him how I presented—how I came across. Honesty, I implored, no holding back. Boy, did he run with that!

He started with my image. Apparently I dressed like a man. According to Jon my trendy but practical loafers were a man repellent. Paired with my button down blouses and baggy trousers (hey, they were fashionable!), I was playing into my masculine but good.

Next came the truth about my persona—cool, independent, intimidating. It basically screamed, "I can take care of myself, thank you very much. No man need apply." Ouch and W.O.W. did I ever need to fem up fast! Jon's words were piercing but they also spoke to my soul. I knew he was right.

My memory conjured a final scene with Stephano, his words echoing in my mind: "You don't need me," he said matter-of-factly. "*She* makes me feel wonderful, like a man." His words had cut my heart to the quick—of course I needed him, why couldn't he see that? With Jon's help I understood—the independent veneer had masked my needs. I was sad to see whom I had become, how far I'd strayed from my feminine, and how uncomfortable vulnerability made me.

Even though Jon's critique stung, I felt liberated. Finally I "got it." "This is fabulous!" I thought. "I have direction. It's time to get out of my man boots and back into my stilettos!"

Viva la Reinvention!

By this point reclaiming myself was a thrilling proposition. Not only could I find my feminine voice, I could unearth the woman I'd buried so long ago and say hello to that sensual and vulnerable part of me that I knew existed. Not all of these feelings and thoughts were at a conscious level, I only knew my soul was calling out to me—and I was listening. I trusted my guidance and declared with passion, "I, Sherri Nickols, commit to reclaiming and connecting to my feminine essence!"

And that was that. I had no idea how transformative my next actions would be but I can tell you in no uncertain terms, they were life changing.

The next day, I was a woman on a mission: buying a whole new wardrobe suitable for a starring role in *Sex and the City*—body-hugging tops, skirts with slits, sexy high heels, fabulous accessories.

But truthfully, even though I was off to a good start, I soon found out mustering the courage to create a new look and actually owning it are two separate things entirely! When the reality set in that I would now have to wear those get-ups in public—and on dates—I began to sweat. I had no idea how to do the dating scene after so many years away. Talk about a fish out of water! I mean, I'd spent the last decade covering cleavage, wearing trendy yet classic and conservative clothing. How was I *ever* going to pull this off?

My solution? I decided to choose a role model to help me develop my new persona. I wasn't looking to become her, just hoping to capture the flavor of her image. I chose a friend who had it going on—she was a "woman" in every sense of the word. It was certainly a stretch for me but I focused on her strong attributes of femininity, confidence, vulnerability, charm, and allure. She reveled in dressing like a woman, being seen and admired.

It was quite overwhelming initially, like learning how to drive for the first time. But just as you eventually get comfortable with the side streets and are able to ramp up to the highway, I slowly gained the confidence to be seen as a woman.

Around this same time, a single voluptuous friend of mine in her mid 30's turned me on to a fabulous secret of her dating success. She confided that whenever she felt insecure about her weight or look, she would swing into her walk all the more and say to herself, "I am a sexy, beautiful woman." She swore it was this affirming attitude and celebration of self that would turn every head in the room.

That made me realize it wasn't just about the wrapping but what's *inside* the wrapping, emanating out, that's even more important.

So I began my inner work. And after several months I had to know—was I successful in developing and integrating my feminine essence?

A Kiss and a Prayer

"Sometimes our light goes out but is blown again into flame

by an encounter with another human being. Each of us owes the deepest thanks to those who have rekindled this inner light."

—Albert Schweitzer

Enter my very own "Mr. Big." You know the type, the guy that makes you giddy all over, the manly man—strong, handsome, kind…and a bit unpredictable. And there was this undeniable soul connection—a comfort and familiarity, like we had danced together forever—a feeling I never had with my ex.

But there were also a few little obstacles—like he was a workaholic professional, separated with 50% custody of his children, and extremely guarded. Seriously, getting to this man was like accessing the Oval Office. Even though there were lots of sparks between us he hid behind his fortress of self-defense mechanisms. I knew I would have to do something crazy creative to get him out of his cocoon.

My girlfriends and I spent many gab sessions scheming up strategies. Finally the perfect opportunity presented itself: my friends were putting together a treasure hunt at the Museum of Contemporary Art, and they brilliantly suggested I invite him. I know what you're thinking, *Mr. Me is back,* but hear me out. I was recovering from an emotionally devastating divorce and desperately needed a fun distraction. Exploring and stretching my creativity and femininity was crucial.

That said, I knew I couldn't send my Mr. Big the basic boring invitation. No, it had to be an intriguing presentation full of mystery and surprise—something tempting that would take his focus from his jam-packed life and pique his curiosity.

Holding that desire and intention, I almost instantly received the most divinely inspired vision. And just like that, my creativity and inhibitions became unleashed. As I set about gathering my goodies, I was filled with a bliss I had never known. It seemed like I was riding on the wings of God! I involved a few of my fab friends and together we had a ball creating an incredibly adventurous and flirty invite.

Treasure hunts are all about the mystery and intrigue, so I fed that feeling with a container that was very "Message in a Bottle." I filled it with sand, seashells, and colorful Mardi Gras beads...wrote the invite on musty medieval parchment paper and burned the edges...rolled and stuffed it partway into the bottle...tied it off with a piece of weathered rope...entwined a pirate patch...placed it in a crate filled with dried seaweed... and placed a note atop the greens as the final touch: "An Adventure Awaits You..."

I sent it to his office with a kiss and a prayer. Thus began one of the most important romances of my life.

Even though Mr. Big was totally intrigued by my surprise package he was unable to attend due to work obligations... or so he said. Not having fully recovered from the fallout of my marriage, I let my insecurities and trust issues get the best of me. I found myself wondering if he really had a work commitment or was just blowing me off. Especially since he said he wanted to meet for coffee soon...but soon never came. As fate would have it, after about a month, I was given another divinely inspired idea and the courage to give it one last-ditch effort. I figured if God was giving me these ideas, who was I to ignore them? Besides, I was in the discovery stages of my inner enchantress and discovering that my feminine creative expression brought me great joy.

This time I put together a coffee-themed invitation with a clock. I included a note, "The clock is ticking...how long does a girl have to wait for a cup of coffee?" Again I shared my adventure with one of my closest gal pals; we giggled and brainstormed and her added creativity made this invite brilliant with a "P.S. Don't let the coffee get cold!"

Sweet success! Mr. Big called and asked me out. I felt I could fly to the moon I was so happy. But I was also very nervous—it was time to test the truth of my feminine make-over. I called in my precious posse of friends for a powwow—I desperately needed a pep talk and some savvy *fashionista* eyes! So I whipped up a pitcher of frothy margaritas, blared a killer Barry White CD, and began to saunter my most delicious date ensembles.

With their help the perfect outfit was chosen, my confidence bolstered, and my courage kindled. My girlfriends' unwavering love and support brought tremendous joy to my journey making my transformation possible. They were truly my angels.

When the big day arrived and I dressed for my date I felt fully feminine from the inside out. I slipped into a long black skirt with side slits, a body-hugging lilac top and strappy, sexy black sandals. With the help of some fabulous foundations that shifted and shaped me into a woman I didn't recognize, I was ready for my close-up!

The first date with Mr. Big was magical—the kind of night you never want to end. Our connection ignited my creativity and I started having vision after vision of unique ways to add fun, mystery, and adventure into relationships. Little did I know it at the time, but this new romance sparked the beginning of my life's work and ultimately this book.

Birth of the "Romance-Capade™"

As my romantic invitation concept evolved, I began designing themed surprise packages for friends who wanted to spark up their relationships. To my delight, my idea caught on like wildfire.

During this time I was sharing my romantic escapades with two of my closest girlfriends, Patti and Maureen whom I also worked with. Having been there for me and seeing firsthand what I went through on a daily basis with my divorce they were my biggest cheerleaders, applauding every action I took to ensure my transformation.

My experience made them realize the need to nurture their own marriages since Patti was a newlywed and Maureen a few years into her nuptials. Subsequently, our lunch breaks turned into the ultimate "girl talk" sessions, a safe haven for us to collectively help each other deal with and face our own hidden insecurities and desires about life, love and everything in between.

These conversations evolved into creative collaboration. Together we brainstormed fun and sexy "Romance-Capades" that blew our partners away and ignited our love lives. We began to feel like "love gurus"!

One of the most important realizations I had about summoning the courage to step outside of my comfort zone was that it blessed my life in five phenomenal ways:

1) It increased my confidence and taught me how to access my joy for life.
2) It helped me connect with and unleash my divine feminine essence—living fully in my playful and creative Self-expression.
3) It brought the meaning of friendship to a whole new level—trusting, bonding, creating, collaborating and laughing...and laughing...and laughing.
4) It opened me to new possibilities allowing me to

experience an amazing love.

5) It brought thrilling, fun adventures that enriched my life far beyond what I could have ever imagined.

I discovered that by empowering yourself to unleash hidden desires not only are you honoring your true feminine voice, you are also establishing, expanding and evolving all important relationships in your life, especially your relationship with YOU. I felt I was on to something big!

Wishing to share this concept with all women to help them unlock their sensuality and secret desires, and enrich the bond with both their men and their girlfriends, my business, Unleash Your Inner Sparkle, was born (www.UnleashYourInnerSparkle.com).

So began home romance parties where intrigued and interested women would gather to learn how to mix things up in their relationships. And just as my posse of gal pals and I delighted in designing sensual escapades together, these women also cheered each other on. It was clear they enjoyed being together, supporting each other, sharing something new together, hanging together and being a part of each other's lives. Just like *Sex and the City* suggests, we women love any excuse to escape our crazy busy lives to have some fun with our girlfriends!

Within the realm of these romantic soirees, instead of getting together to complain about their lives and lovers, the women were encouraged to shift into a new mindset. They were empowered to take responsibility for their romantic wants and needs, to use their imagination to design frisky frolics taking their relationships to new levels of intimacy. It was very inspiring to see the shifts. I helped countless women discover their inner desires and plan their passionate trysts. It was exhilarating to share their success stories and hear the excitement in their voices. They loved how "womanly" they felt and how the romantic adventures brought such renewed sparks to their relationships. They were surprised how much fun they had planning their Romance-Capades and a new sense of pride and confidence couldn't help but spill into their lives. Many shared how they were initially timid and unsure of themselves—fearing an unfavorable response from their mate. But encouragement coupled with pinky swears with me and their friends pushed them forward. When it came right down to it, mustering the moxie to create a new flavor in their relationship was as much about spicing up their love life as it was about having a juicy story to share with their supportive group of girlfriends. How I loved this new community of Sparkling Soul Sisters that was emerging!

As my work evolved I met more and more women who were suffering from feminine famine, and just as I had during my soul-squelching marriage, they were sourcing their power through an adoption of masculine traits. I also witnessed in these women a lot of emotional suppression, denial of anger, disconnection from sensual Self and desires, and concealment of their beautiful light. I became aware of the real fear and limitations most women live with that prevent them from blossoming into the fullness of their feminine essence. Consequently, even though these fabulous females craved deep connection with their partners, they didn't have a clue how to make that happen. They overwhelmingly requested detailed instruction, and thus this book was born.

So beauty, get ready to dust off your diamond and let that sexy, sparkling woman that is *you* shine.

Introduction

Ever wonder where that radiant, fun-loving, sexy woman went? Or ask yourself, "When did my life get so routine? Where did the joy go? Where did the *PASSION* go? When did I lose my *Self*?"

You are not alone. Millions of women ask themselves these questions every day.

Chances are your love life isn't as delicious as it used to be either. Would you say it's boring, dull or even non-existent?

Again, you're not alone. A third of all marriages are only "semi-happy," experts say, filled with low-level conflict and ambivalence. Hardly the picture of passionate, soul-to-soul connection, is it?

If you're over 40 and single, you may be yearning for a mate but looking for love in all the wrong places...or hiding out at home or work, afraid to look at all.

Here's the good news: the secret to revitalizing your Self and revving up your love life is YOU! Once you connect with your essential sparkling essence you'll be able to create the love life you crave.

Welcome to *Sexy and Sparkling After 40*—this book is dedicated to helping women get their "sparkle" on. This means unearthing and owning the diamond in you, falling madly in love with yourself, feeling sexy at any age, learning how to laugh and love with total freedom so you can transform your life.

It's for all you working women who have conquered your career but live with a personal life that is less than luscious. You've lost your Self along the way and have forgotten how to have fun, surrender to pleasure and express your creative, passionate essence. If you're in a relationship you've forgotten how to blend romantic adventure into the mix.

This book is also for you "Super Moms"—off to the races from the moment your feet hit the ground in the morning. Doing, doing, doing for everyone but yourself—consumed with guilt when you do take time for you. Like the career gals you're out of touch with both your fabulous factor and your sexy Self. And you know it's time to get them back.

Just how do you do that? It's actually very simple. Happily, it revolves around a woman's best friend: DIAMONDS.

Seriously, have you ever noticed how similar women are to diamonds? When you think of this queen of all gems, what comes to mind? A beautiful, brilliant, sparkling, clear, multi-faceted jewel with incredible strength and inherent value, right? Voila, women *are* like diamonds!

But here's the rub. When we are disconnected from our diamond power, our true authentic essence, it's easy to allow life experiences to cloud and confuse our perception of Self, to dim our light, to affect the way we value and love ourselves. This blocks us from getting the love we crave and deserve.

If you are silently stuffing your needs and waiting for someone else to fulfill your desires, you are giving away your power and probably resenting it, to boot. Not a happy place to be. Yet again, you are not alone.

Let's face it, a relationship can look fine on the surface and seem like it's working in many ways, yet one or both partners are plagued by a nagging feeling of dissatisfaction. Rather than face the specter of change, they numb themselves and sink into denial and resignation. Surprisingly, few marriages fail because of an intolerable situation or dramatic betrayal. Rather, the most troubled couples simply stop communicating and drift apart.

After working with women clients for over 10 years, I've heard many a common complaint. "My relationship is stuck in a rut." "Romance, schomance, I might as well have married my brother." "I want a deep intimate connection with the man of my dreams—why is that so difficult to find?"

These are the vexed voices of women just like you—successful, powerful, and attractive. And like yours, their pain is very real, very personal and very deep.

The majority of us are stuck in old patterns and beliefs that no longer serve us. Or we're so used to being aggressive in the workplace that we've forgotten how to doff the man boots and slip on our sexy stilettos.

The result is frustration, anger and loneliness.

The solution is easy: love your *Self* first and foremost.

I discovered this simple but elusive truth the hard way. After going through a devastating divorce, I spent a long time digging for, discovering and excavating my lost diamond essence—then *polishing, polishing, polishing* until it sparkled anew. (If you haven't already, read "How It All Began" for my personal story…warts and all.)

As I journeyed back to me, I paid attention to what worked. Visualizing my future, getting clear on what I really wanted, discovering my passions, bonding with my circle of angel friends, learning to laugh and play again, daring to express my passionate creativity…these were all steps toward reclaiming my diamond power. Once again my light shined through.

I wanted to share what I learned with every woman. It became my passion to help others avoid the anguish I'd gone through in getting back my Self. Through my process I created the SPARKLE System™ presented in this book. I've used it to help countless women find their diamond power and develop Self-love.

With this seven-step system you'll not only rediscover who you really are, but you'll be given the tips, tools and strategies to regain your value, your vibrancy, your mojo and your joy. You'll learn how to live from your heart instead of your head, reconnect with your feminine power, awaken your sensuality, and create a support system with your girlfriends. You'll learn how to love more, play more, and Be more, so you can build the life of your dreams.

This book is all about helping you discover and own the diamond in you. As I teach you how to love yourself, you'll be inspired to honor you, go within, dig deep to uncover your buried desires and express them freely empowering YOU to "sparkle" and enjoy more love in your life. This is the true voice of your soul.

And guess what? Self-transformation doesn't need to be hard and painful. You may have some tough times, but you don't need to endure an endless dark night of the soul. So many gurus and spiritual teachers lead us to believe we have to stay in that scary place a long time. Nonsense! Self-discovery and renewal can be light and fun—especially when you embrace the SPARKLE System™.

The first section of this book is all about the SPARKLE System™. First there's an overview of all seven steps. This will give you a sense of the process as a whole, although you can mix and match the steps, or focus on the one you need the most. Each step is designed to stand on its own as well as work with the others.

Before covering each step in detail, in Chapter 2 we'll identify common behaviors and beliefs that dim our dazzle. Next we'll explore the precious gift of friendship. Chapter 3 shows you how to celebrate, renew—or create for the first time—a warm circle of soul sisters you can turn to for laughter, loving advice, and mutual support.

Then we'll explore each step one-by-one. Stories of clients and friends, women just like you, bring each step to life. These stories show how real women dealt with the challenges that faced them as they shed old behaviors, adopted positive habits, and brought more zest and joy into their lives.

Once your mojo is flowing again, you'll be rewarded with your very own Passport to Passion. This section of the book gives you 15 sizzling "Romance-Capades™" to rev up your love life. If you're in a relationship, you can use these sexy adventures to unleash your creative expression and play out all your romantic desires. If you're single, these saucy escapades will help you visualize yourself with passion and courage, so that when the man of your dreams shows up you'll be ready!

Keep an open mind and heart while reading, and if at any time you find yourself feeling a bit nervous, take that to mean this book is exactly what you need to catapult you into the life you desire. Have a journal handy to write about anything coming up making you uncomfortable.

Sexy and Sparkling After 40 shares how to:

- Love yourself—you cannot give what you don't have
- Connect with your feminine power
- Increase confidence
- Improve self-esteem
- Create a support system with your girlfriends
- Overcome limiting beliefs and patterns
- Awaken your sensuality and boost your sex appeal
- Communicate from the heart
- Flirt with life
- Reclaim your playful, sexy spirit
- Balance your masculine and feminine energies
- Stand in your power *without* power struggles
- Create fun, romantic adventures to rekindle your relationship or magnetize a new one

Since you've read this far I know one very important thing about you…that you deeply desire to get your sparkle back and find intimacy, playfulness and connection but you haven't yet figured out how to capture them.

I honor you for reaching out and I am delighted you've found *Sexy and Sparkling After 40*—a book that gives you a road map back to your essential diamond essence. Along the journey you'll fall madly in love with yourself and transform your life—living, laughing and loving with total freedom.

My goal is to empower one million women to fall head over heels in love with themselves and get their sparkle on. Are you in? Girlfriend, you are on your way. Turn the page and let your excavation begin!

The SPARKLE System™

Chapter 1

Get Your Sparkle On!

Would you like to know the secret to feeling sexy at any age? To feel so comfortable in your skin you confidently walk into any situation knowing your radiance is magnetizing? If you're like most women over 40 you're spending a fortune and looking everywhere for this Holy Grail when in fact it doesn't cost a dime and resides right in your backyard. Ready to get the skinny? Sexiness comes from your inner light, your sparkle. As Marianne Williamson says, "Charisma is a sparkle in people that money can't buy. It's an invisible energy with visible effects." Available to you at anytime, it's the key to living *la dolce vita!*

So you might be asking, "if it's within me, *how did I lose 'it' and how do I get 'it' back?"*

Yes indeed, how did this sparkle slip away? The truth is somewhere along the way while you were racing to do everything everyone told you would make you happy, successful, and accomplished, you not only lost your way, you disconnected from your radiant Self.

And what about your love life? If you're single, is it by choice or do you bounce from relationship to relationship letting your fear that you'll never meet the man of your dreams steal your light? If you're involved, has your once-passionate relationship disintegrated into a platonic partnership filled with resentment and loneliness leaving you feeling blah and thinking, "Is this *it?*"

Sadly you're not alone. There's a sea of attractive, intelligent and caring women, just like you, hiding their disheartened, disconnected, and disappointed feelings—most of all from themselves.

Yet now you've reached a point where you have to admit your reality is a far cry from the beautiful life you had once envisioned. The overwhelm of daily demands, the never-ending to-do list, taking care of everyone but yourself, a challenging career, all the doing vs. being has left you feeling and looking more like a diamond in the rough than a goddess lit by her inner glow.

What's more, owning your radiance and stepping into "feminine power" has been a bit confusing for forward-thinking females ever since the '60s, causing not only a loss of connection, balance, and intimate bonding in relationships, but a loss of personal happiness as well. With very few powerful feminine role models for us to emulate, "power" has been misinterpreted as masculine. The art and pleasure of being a woman got lost, and the idea of playfulness flew out the window—along with romantic adventure.

Does this describe you? Would you say you're tired of living like this and deeply desire to look radiant, live with passion and feel *alive*? Then, instead of escaping into the latest Nora Roberts romance novel decide right now that you're going to be the leading lady in your own life story! But *mamma mia,* where to begin, right?

No matter how much you want a closely connected, intimate relationship you don't have a clue how to make that happen. I hear you! At one time, I was in the exact same position. What's worse, I didn't even know I didn't know until my 13-year relationship crumbled. I was so focused on achieving the material goals of our marriage, I blinded myself to the signs that my husband was leading a double life with a woman in another state. When the news of his marital infidelity surfaced, imagine my devastation when he justified his action by saying his new girlfriend had the playful, feminine spirit I *used* to have. Ouch!

Feeling shocked, powerless and lost, I wandered into the bathroom and looked in the mirror. "Who have you become?" I asked as tears burned down my face. I fell into a pitiful pile on the floor, realizing that in trying to do everything I had abandoned my true Self and lost it all.

This sudden, unwanted reality was ripping me apart. Past choices had cost me dearly. Here I was, heading into my 40s, feeling dull, unattractive, insecure and single again! Was my life over? If my husband left me for a younger woman, wouldn't every man think I was too old? It must mean I'm not enough, not desirable. Would any man ever want me again? And then there was the glaring issue of the clock ticking—how was I ever going to meet someone, fall in love and have a baby within my sliver of a window? I was so scared and so lost.

A new important choice was now at hand. Sink or swim. And so it was, at that moment, I declared I would swim like a champ and do whatever it took to enter my 40s as sparkling as I could be, connected to my sensuality and feeling fully alive!

First and foremost, it required that I honestly look at the relationship. The truth is, I had been living primarily in my masculine energy, trying to control all the outcomes. Big mistake, as Julia Roberts would say, BIG mistake. Take it from me, two men in a heterosexual marriage doesn't work!

So take a minute and consider your truth. What are your actions costing you? If you made a conscious choice to live in your empowered feminine state how would your life and relationship benefit?

This is a good time to mention the prologue, "How it All Began." Did you read it? If not, you'll want to go back now and look through it thoroughly because it sets the stage for the premise and promise of this book.

Decide Who You Want to Be

Starting now, decide who you want to be. If you're like me you'll decide you want to find and own YOU. Having lost touch with who you are, or never knowing, can make this a challenging excavation. You will need plenty of shovels to dig deep, helping you remember. Invest in your spiritual growth, join or form support groups, find out what activities make you feel good, take up yoga, travel, and enjoy time with friends. In other words, take action! When you discover what brings you joy your love life will transform.

I'll let you in on a little secret…the key to a life full of passion, warmth and soul-to-soul connection is YOU! When you unlock the real you—the amusing, happy, in-love-with-life sensual woman who adores herself—you will mesmerize your man, and everyone in your world for that matter.

Being grounded in your own greatness and expressing it with

genuine confidence is intoxicating for men. Whether you're single and looking or coupled up in a rut, you'll be positively irresistible. Woohooo!

Quite by accident I found the key that unlocked my truth while flipping through *Vogue* magazine. When I was in the process of reinventing myself I started looking through fashion magazines because I had even lost touch with what style I liked. I had been dressing to please my husband, who was big into fashion and liked me to dress trendy—not always feminine.

One day, I came across the most exquisite pair of Manolo Blahnik high-heeled sandals I had ever seen. I fell in love! They were soft metallic gold with jeweled straps and they screamed sexy with class. I ripped the page out and put it on my bulletin board at my office—they were a constant reminder of the woman I desired to become. More of a loafer girl I yearned to morph into that magnificent jeweled high heel. I wanted to grab the bull by the horns and have the most exciting life imaginable—a life where I could fully embrace my feminine spirit, live my dreams and love with total freedom.

Something shifted in me in that moment. I could see the possibilities. I became aware that I was so attracted to these sparkling stilettos because they were the tangible essence of the self-expression I had been stuffing down year after year.

When I bought those shoes, it was one of the happiest days of my life. Although they cost a fortune, the money never crossed my mind—I knew owning them would help me bring out the truth of who I am. I felt young and hopeful and knew I was starting to find the way back to me again.

What shoe are you? Loafer? Stiletto? Do you wear the stiletto hoping to hide your masculine traits? If you are the loafer but drawn to the beautiful heel, know that your passionate personality is in there. It just needs some help coming out!

The Road to Reconnection

The first step on your journey is back to your birthright because the truth is, who you are, at your core, is a magnificent sparkling gem. What I realized on my quest is that women are like diamonds. We're strong, beautiful, brilliant, dazzling, multifaceted, resilient and valuable. Just like a diamond, as we endure the high pressures of our life we make more fabulous facets and increase our worth.

Finding the road back to your feminine diamond essence is easier than you might think. However, you'll need to identify and give up your distractions. They are toxic to a life of happiness. This means no more saying "yes" to every request that comes your way. Let your drama queen friend cry on someone else's shoulder. Set boundaries with your kids, mate, boss, and anyone else who crosses the line. Let go of the rescue role. And trade some of your daily to-do-list time for a few pampering pleasures.

Sound scary? It can be if you're not used to standing in your diamond power.

As women, we not only need to know how to connect with our feminine essence, our innate juiciness, but also how to let it rise to the surface and spill out so we can feel sensual and fully alive.

One of the ways this happens for me is stepping out into nature. I remember one magical summer morning I was hiking up a hill and came face to face with a crepe myrtle tree. Have you *ever* had the pleasure? From its multiple curvaceous limbs climbing up and out of the earth to its delicate tissue-like flowers blanketing the branches in soft shades of pink, it is the most powerful expression of femininity I have ever laid my eyes upon. This particular morning the petals were swaying from a light breeze creating a sense of flirtation and seduction. What an amazing floral fountain of sensual energy. I drank it in realizing this gorgeous gift of nature exemplifies women. And how!

As I continued on my hike I could not get this tree out of my mind. I was obsessed, so much so I changed course so that I could go back and be in its presence. I felt excitement, urgency; my legs could not carry me fast enough.

Once there, my heart cracked wide open and tears of love and bliss streamed down my face. It was not lost on me that the allure of this crepe myrtle was in its divine Beingness, its authentic natural state. It hadn't chased me down, tried to sell me something, or gone out of its way to please me to get my appreciation. It was just BEING in its God-given beauty.

And in its Beingness, it had connected to, awakened and unleashed my soul's feminine essence, reminding me of who I am. This was a fantastic lesson showing the unparalleled power in Being rather than Doing. It is in this state that you allow people to see the real you.

I started thinking about my clients and friends and the women I encounter—all searching for what they can "do" to make themselves more special, more unique, more attractive. The truth is, we are perfect as we are, and when we sit in the fullness of our raw feminine power we are irresistible.

For most of us this fruitless, never-ending search began as children, when we learned certain behaviors to get love and acceptance from our parents. Thus started the vicious cycle and unhealthy patterns. Next comes looking for love and acceptance from our friends, and then from the men and the partners we want to attract. Over the course of our life, we learn to modulate who we are, twisting ourselves into pretzels to be who we think others want us to be. Tragically, we begin to forget who we are. We forget about our divine magnificence. Talk about not living our truth!

Trying to fit into a box when you are a circle is dangerous and never works to your alluring advantage. When you work so hard to BE something you're not, in order to get something you want, your body goes into rebellion—you're not living authentically so stress, anxiety, and anger rear their ugly heads.

Even if you do get what you think you want, it will blow up in your face down the road because you are not living in integrity. You're sacrificing your truth.

So how do you recapture the Self-love you had before you bought into the false beliefs and doubts about being anything other than whole and complete?

You can turn this vicious cycle around by discovering what brings you joy in life and staying connected to it, living with integrity and honoring your truth.

Can you see why it's so important to know who you are? It's time to acknowledge your inherent beauty, embrace with gratitude your womanhood, honor and respect your divine light, and wake up the playful, fun, adventurous woman in you!

When you give yourself permission to live in this radiant state you will be able to attract all the goodies of life. There will always be obstacles and challenges in life, but the goal is to have the tools to help you regroup easily and get back to your dazzling Self. Once you have your diamond tools you can retrieve and polish your stunning sparkle with consistent and conscious actions.

To make it easy for you to wipe the sludge off your shine, here is a proven seven-step formula that my clients, friends, and I have all used to renew our radiance. Fittingly, it spells out S.P.A.R.K.L.E.

S...See Your Bright Future

The first step in the SPARKLE system is to gain clarity about your life. Figure out what you want and how you want your life to look. If you hang on to past victories or victimizations and allow them to rule your life you will stay stuck and miserable. The key to happiness is moving forward with a clear vision.

SEE YOUR FUTURE Tip

One of the best ways to get clear is to first express what you don't want. Begin by taking a piece of paper and dividing it in half vertically. On the top left column write, "What I don't want" and on the top right, "What I do want." Start on the left with what you know you don't want. Make the list as long and detailed as possible. Once you are done, systematically go through each undesirable thing and write what you do want adjacent to it in the right column. Cross out the left column. Then take a fresh piece of paper, title it "My Bright Future," and list only the items from the right column. Review it daily. This is one of the easiest techniques you can use to get clear about the life that awaits you!

P...Pinpoint Your Passions

Passion is that effusive energy that screams, "I'm ALIVE." It brings vibrancy to your entire being showcasing your gorgeous goddess spirit. Passion seduces everyone in its path with its fiery flames so if you want to captivate your man simply figure out what ignites your soul.

PASSION Tip

Make a list of 10 activities that you're passionate about and title it "My Passion Plan". Embracing those things that bring you joy will empower the enchantress in you. You will become delightfully aware that you no longer need to exhaust yourself with all the DOING. That's the beauty of it: connecting and activating your spark will bring excitement and love back into your life. Print your list and cut it to the size of a business card. Take this to a copy center and have it laminated. Make three copies: carry one in your wallet, put one next to your bed or in the bathroom, and place the last one in your office where you will see it. Do one of these activities every day and you'll see your life and relationship start to sizzle again. Goddess of fire, ignite!

A...Adjust Your Attitude

A positive attitude is more than a cheery disposition—it's connecting, owning and embracing the fullness of who you are. It's the brilliant mastery of recognizing the negative aspects that you face, and choosing instead to focus on the hope and opportunity available within every situation. A good attitude energetically attracts fantastic situations into your life—a whirlwind of good fortune and positive experiences creating a renewal of sorts. It's approaching life with grace and gratitude and living in expansion—trying new things, exploring new thoughts, embarking on new adventures.

ATTITUDE Tip

I love the story about Marilyn Monroe walking down the street with one of her girlfriends clad in a headscarf and dark glasses, seemingly invisible. Her gal pal was dumbfounded. Marilyn, the hottest sex symbol around, was getting no gawks! She commented on it and Marilyn simply replied, "That's because I'm in my Norma Jean zone—but watch this." Then she took off her glasses, pulled down her scarf and started sashaying down the avenue with her famous Marilyn persona. Within seconds every man's head was turning (and I'm sure several envious women as well!). Just goes to show, a great attitude about Self can be learned successfully!

R...Renew Your Relationship With YOU!

If you are like most women, you feel guilty about taking time to refuel your energy. Yet if your intention is to be able to give to your loved ones, the only way you can do this is to be kind and loving to yourself first. That is the most loving thing you can do for the people you care about. In truth, the most significant relationship you'll ever have is with *yourself.* Your happiness and capacity to give and receive love stems from how you treat yourself. Next is your ability to reach out and authentically relate to other people. When you are able to do this, without an agenda, everything you desire in life, everything you yearn for, will manifest—the support, the right people, and wonderful opportunities.

RELATIONSHIP Tip

Imagine you are a big, beautiful pitcher of lemonade and there are several glasses surrounding you that want to be filled up with your delicious drink. These represent your mate, kids, job, friends, family, etc. As you gladly fill each cup, eventually you become an empty pitcher and have nothing left to give. Yet their thirst can't be quenched and they continue to ask for more. This is a pivotal point. If you attempt to accommodate their needs before replenishing your pitcher they will not be satisfied and you will feel frustrated, inadequate and exhausted from the effort of trying to give when you have nothing left. The key is to recognize when you are depleted, take the time to nurture yourself first, and fully fill yourself back up. Then you'll be able to pour more love easily and effortlessly.

K...Know Who You Are

Getting back to YOU means living authentically in your truth—standing for what you believe in, unafraid to voice it, proud of who you are at your core. You have a beautiful, intimate bond with your inner self so there is no need to seek external approval or people-please to validate your worth. It means knowing you are a pure reflection of God; as such it is easy to acknowledge your value and honor your essence.

KNOWINGNESS Tip

Do you let people see the real you or do you wear a mask pretending to be someone you're not? If you spend more time trying to satisfy the needs of others so that you'll be liked or loved instead of setting boundaries and taking care of your own needs, you are burying your diamond essence. You'll need to dig your way out, grab the buffer, and start polishing. Soon the fabulous you will shine through!

Get started by asking yourself these three questions:

1) *What am I passionate about?*
2) *What are my strengths and talents?*
3) *What do I value?*

Know and love yourself and watch your world become smitten!

L...Laugh and Play

Laughter is the sunshine of your soul and creates instant connection. You will imprison yourself if you choose to be rigid, stubborn and inflexible. As a woman you have an innate gift of flirtatiousness, playfulness, softness—this is your feminine power. This is your strength! Use it to change the dynamics of an unpleasant situation or to transform those boring moments. Make playtime as important as work time and mom time. You wouldn't blow off a client, would you? So why are you blowing off your need for fun and romantic adventure? Put it in your weekly planner and then do it!

LAUGHTER Tip

Lighten your mood with laughter and playfulness. One way to do this is to come up with silly nicknames for you and your mate to ease tension in communication. Make sure you come up with these together and don't let sarcasm sneak into your tone or it could backfire. Did you know 93% of communication has nothing to do with what you say, but how you say it? Make sure there is playfulness in your voice! For example, if you want to have a heart-to-heart with your man and he's closed off, lean in and lightly say with a smile, "Well, I see the Berlin Wall is up!" By introducing humor, you'll create a safe environment for connection and understanding.

E...Embrace Your Life

Living life fully requires balancing your softness with your power, knowing when to flip from Doing to Being, being open to all that life offers, and letting your love flow. Give yourself permission to rediscover how to play and flirt, be sassy and sensual, and create the love you long for. More importantly, get comfortable with it!

EMBRACE LIFE Tip

If you want a luscious life, YOU need to take the lead. Waiting for others or circumstances to create it for you leads to disappointment, anger and sadness. Reclaim your sparkling, playful spirit by making a conscious choice to be adventurous, daring and wild. Take charge of your life, step outside the box, and free that vibrant, sensual, loving woman within. I've taken so many risks in my life.

Some turned out and others didn't, but they all moved me forward and gave me confidence. I believe our purpose is to experience as much as we can in this life and through it all we grow. It's about approaching life with grace and gratitude and true zest. Embracing life means being open to new ways of Being, new ideas, and new adventure.

Now that you have an overview of the SPARKLE System, get ready to reconnect with your raw feminine power. In the next chapter we'll explore what it looks like to be a sexy and sparkling woman over 40—and the limiting beliefs and behaviors that commonly hold us back. One of them is the notion that we have to do everything on our own. Nonsense! Chapter 3 celebrates female friendship and the extraordinary gifts our girlfriends bring to our life. Chapters 4 through 11 dive deeply into each step of the SPARKLE system. From there you'll claim your Passport to Passion, transporting you to 15 Romance-Capades—saucy adventures that will help you bring all your playful personas to the surface and mesmerize your man. Be willing to embrace a different way of doing things and soon you will be living the life you deserve—as the pleasure loving Italians would say, *la dolce vita!*

Chapter 2

Ways We Lose Our Radiance

Imagine…you've set the mood with alluring red light bulbs. The sultry sounds of "Light My Fire" fill the room. Your sexy velvet panties feel delicious against your skin. Your senses sizzle as you sensually massage your man in front of a roaring fire…you've ignited the flames of his passion by creating an inferno of love. Burn baby, burn!

A woman who is sparkling and sexy after 40 is a woman who is brave enough to step outside her comfort zone and plan a Romance-Capade for her lover like the one above. Not there yet? Don't worry, few of us are, until we reclaim our innate diamond power, our divine, feminine essence.

So what came up for you while reading this steamy scene? Intrigue? Fear? Desire? Shyness?

If you said, "All of the above" you're not alone. The good news is, by the time you finish this book you will have the courage, confidence and playfulness to do this yourself. After learning the SPARKLE System, presented in Chapters 4 through 11, you'll know how to navigate through the sludge, overcome your fears and transform your limiting beliefs so you can live with vibrancy. After you're feeling sexy and sparkling again you'll head into the Passport to Passion section where I give you 15 Romance-Capades— fun, romantic adventures both you and your man will love—to help you explore and express the many facets of your sensual side.

If you're single you can visualize yourself having the confidence and creativity to pull off any of the passionate interludes so when the man of your dreams appears, you're ready!

What's Blocking Your Bliss?

First let's take a look at what caused you to flat-line, derail and lose your sparkle so you can make better choices from here on out.

In the beginning life is all about you. But then you start sacrificing your "me" time to shine in your career, to be the perfect wife or girlfriend, and to cater to your kids. As you get older, whether you're single or in a committed relationship, your needs begin taking a back seat and you start settling for less telling yourself it'll just be this *one* time. Somehow the one time turns into a thousand times burying your needs completely. You wake up one day feeling blind-sided wondering, "how did this happen?" Here's the skinny—this mud slide you've been buried under gained momentum from a river of reasons, like your partner throwing his laundry list of to-do's on you, needy friends consuming your time, kids' busy schedules, aging parents' needs, a demanding career and boss, volunteer work, and all those "well-meaning" friends and family who love to judge and criticize the way you do things—all triggering you to derail and lose your sparkle. Wouldn't it be great to shake it off and shimmer again?

Fortunately, if you choose to empower yourself with insight and awareness, it is possible to make different choices for better outcomes. Remember, Einstein said the definition of insanity is doing the same thing over and over again expecting different results. So get ready. Gather your courage. It's time to do some digging. Get excited because whatever you uncover will not only give you the opportunity to take the sludge off your shine, it will set you free!

Let's start with taking a peek at what's just beneath the surface: disappointment and disenchantment. If you are like millions of women over 40 you may be asking yourself, "Is this *it*?" The life you expected never showed up, you've forgotten who you are, and you don't feel valued. You feel gypped! Big time! There could even be a rage inside of you, but since good girls aren't supposed to get angry it surfaces as depression, anxiety, rigidity, control, or my favorite, the "plastered smile" that keeps you looking perfect but is nothing more than a mask hiding your pain.

Most women had a childhood fantasy of being whisked away by Prince Charming to be protected, loved and cherished; this either crashed and burned or hasn't materialized yet. Or maybe you dreamed of building a business or doing something for humanity and here you sit, middle-aged without having accomplished your goals. Maybe your once-passionate relationship is now platonic and seems to be going nowhere. Perhaps you've created an amazing business that looks good on the outside but is built on lies. You're not walking your talk.

Regardless, the clock is ticking fast and furious, anxiety is mounting, and the sludge sisters—Lonesome, Fearful and Stuck—are dimming your dazzle.

To blind yourself to the obvious you choose to live in la la land, telling yourself everything is fine. Not wanting to deal with the truth you cover your eyes and ears, disregard the red flags, and fool yourself into believing if you just keep on keeping on, you won't be found out and everything will all work out. And maybe it does for a while, but deep down, in the gunges of your soul, you know you're living a lie.

Now you are faced with two choices. Either 'fess up and come clean, allowing yourself to breathe and come alive again, or continue with your fraudulent life, pretending to be someone you are not, pretending you have something you don't, and try to ignore the emptiness that's growing inside, eclipsing your light and diamond power.

Try as you might, there's a deep knowing that there *is* something missing. Your soul longs for more. And the "more" is connection, intimacy and love. The "more" is living in your raw feminine power as the sensual goddess you were born to be. If you're single and still alone you've built up a lot of calluses along the way, but underneath it all your heart is hurt and lonely. Maybe you're overeating to fill the void and avoid the discomfort, or shopping like a wild woman, or drinking or having insignificant sex, or isolating—no matter what your coping mechanism you're settling for a life that is far less than what you deserve.

The true longing of the soul is to be one with others. Reaching out and connecting, rather than staying in your bubble of independence, will bring you the closeness you crave. Sharing and caring, giving and receiving love, that's where the joy comes, the juice.

But before you can develop this deep intimacy with a partner you must first develop it with YOU.

Yet how do you slide into this coveted space when you are sabotaged by disempowering patterns and beliefs and faced with challenges and obstacles every day? It can be a struggle without a plan, which is why I devised the SPARKLE System, to help you navigate the negativity and keep your divine essence blazing brightly. But first, let's shine a light on some common patterns that dim our dazzle.

Radiance Robbers

Remember being young, open and idealistic? Didn't you stand on a soapbox and shout your heartfelt views for the world to hear, feeling totally alive and vibrant? Me too. Then life happened. The next thing you know you're speaking from your head instead of your heart, totally disconnected from your essential essence. Your face becomes a mask to hide your hurt, the walls go up to protect your shattered soul and you exhaust yourself trying to control everything in your path—like *that's* going to keep you safe and empowered. Right. Similar to a blood transfusion you've replaced every ounce of passion and courage with unhappiness and fear. You might be asking yourself, "How did this happen?"

There are countless scenarios that can contribute to losing your passion, but the 13 snatchers described below played a big part in my own life and also in those of the women I coach. Are any of these culprits robbing you of your radiance as well?

Approval Seeking

Jane, a successful career woman, had what others would consider a beautiful life. With an exciting career in the apparel industry she was able to buy a home on the beach in California, drive a convertible Jaguar, travel to exotic places and dress like a glamour queen. She kept herself extraordinarily busy with an active social life and was close with her family. Yet Jane was lonely.

She had created a life that looked good from the outside to cover her huge fear and insecurity that she was not enough. She didn't value herself so she sought attention through her lifestyle to prove her worth. The only hitch, it didn't work in the long run. Until Jane, at her core, felt valuable, she was on a hamster wheel to impress others so they would, in turn, be impressed by her, making her feel special and important. Exhausting!

After working with me she realized her underlying motivation for just about everything she did as a child was to gain approval. This set her up in her adult life to seek her value through external validation. Searching for outside approval to give you your value will suck the ever-loving life out of you.

Jane started to notice she took everything personally. When other people's comments or actions didn't validate her worth or importance, she became angry and explosive. She was being triggered by her core belief that she's not enough.

Like Jane, many people don't see their innate value and seek validation from external sources. This can make you feel needy, lonely, judged, unsupported and invisible. It can even cause you to be suspicious and distrustful when someone does validate you. Before you know it you're an island, doing everything on your own, feeling overwhelmed, resentful and empty. You've hit a dangerous point, crossing the line into a more masculine presence—creating the opposite of what your heart really wants—connection and love!

I also used to seek external validation—especially from my mom—but one day I experienced a miracle that changed my relationship with her forever. About to enter into another no-win conversation, I left the house and asked God for help. I was at my wits end and prayed in earnest, "Please God, tell me, what would love do?" I instantly felt my heart open and expand with love and compassion for my mom. I was able to put myself in her shoes and feel her sadness and disappointment with life. I immediately understood it was necessary to get out of my self-absorption so I could see with a compassionate heart.

When I re-entered the house I noticed the air felt different. Before I had a chance to say anything my mom explained in a very heartfelt way why she was so upset. It was absolutely amazing and life-changing to see how my big shift created just as big of a change in her. I invite you to ask the same question the next time you find yourself in a challenging situation—it's your freedom card!

The big lesson for Jane was realizing she lost her power when waiting for others to approve of her and define her value. This no-win situation, she acknowledged, was diminishing her glow. Her new approach was to practice Self-love and honor her inner divinity. She recognized if she didn't see her magnificence, others wouldn't either—they would simply mirror her thoughts and fears back to her. Your subconscious is always working to fulfill your core beliefs. If you believe you are not valuable, like Jane did, unconsciously you will set up situations to prove your subconscious is right.

After completing a few exercises with me, Jane began to understand that her very existence made her inherently valuable. When she owned it, others felt it and started to value her as well. She became more focused on her alignment with her authentic self and less on what other people thought of her. As she did so she was also able to let go of defining her worth based on her material success. As she fell in love with herself, others naturally became magnetized to her radiance.

Fear of Rejection

Perhaps you want to reach out and express your desires and feelings but are afraid you'll be rejected. If, as a child, you expressed your feelings and weren't taken seriously, were made fun of or weren't supported, you may have a fear you'll be hung out to dry.

What this really means is you don't feel safe being vulnerable. The possibility of rejection often carries the meaning, *I'm not lovable,* and this is more painful than the passionless life you live.

Julie had this complex. She was a gorgeous woman who came to one of my first romance parties. Even though she looked confident she was resistant to try any of the Romance-Capades because she was terrified her husband would laugh at her. I finally persuaded her to start on the mild side with some sexy new lingerie.

Shortly afterward she and her husband took an overnight trip. When he went into the bathroom that evening she quickly put on her pretty new bra and panties and lay seductively on the bed with the lights out and a few candles burning. When hubby came out he was beyond haaapppy! Julie had never done anything like this before and her beauty mesmerized him. With his positive reaction she was able to release a good deal of her fear. The next time I saw her she had clearly blossomed and was eager to try something else.

In my studies I came across a great question to ask yourself when fearful of rejection: If you reach out and get rejected you are no worse off than before you asked, *so what have you got to lose?* This has become my staple question to clients and myself when facing this fear. The obvious answer is "nothing," so forge ahead, dear heart, with courage and determination!

Fear

More encompassing than being afraid of rejection, we can also slip on an overriding fear. If you've been hurt in the past you might be terrified to open up again. Exposing that very tender side of you and showing vulnerability can be scary. But opening up and exposing who you are and being who you are is the only way you will have the love-filled life you want. Whether that means a passionate relationship with the man of your dreams or a love affair with life, take the first step and face it head on.

When you are fearful of trusting others with the secrets of your heart you will keep yourself from having the very thing you want...intimacy, connection and love. You may be frightened of others knowing such intimate details of your life—thinking they will betray you or use it against you. When you live in that protective state, you may think you are getting away with something but in truth it's just another way to separate and isolate, cheating yourself of connection. It's a trick we play to rob ourselves of love.

It's said there are only two emotions—love and fear. So if you aren't feeling love, you can be certain there's a fear lurking. Be forewarned, fear is smart. It often fools you by showing up as something that doesn't look like fear. For example, you make a beautiful and romantic dinner for you and your man but he gets caught up at work and doesn't let you know he'll be late. As you sit waiting for him to arrive, all dolled up, candles lit, and Marc Antoine filling the air space, anger starts to bubble up and you begin to feel disrespected. If you have the courage to dig deeper you'll hear a fearful little voice saying you aren't important or a priority in his life. Your real fear is that you aren't enough and he might leave you. Anger is a great cover for fear—it's important to look under your fiery thoughts and discover the root so you can pull it up, heal it and plant some love seeds instead.

Compromising Your Needs

Are you hyper-vigilant to other people's needs? To the point where you put your needs on the back burner and give their needs top priority? Say you get up in the morning with a bunch of to do's and your sister calls with a favor—do you put your list aside to help her?

Then you get a call from a distressed friend who is having another crisis and needs to vent. Do you tell her it's not a good time or do you spend an hour listening and offering support, putting your own agenda on hold?

Next you get a call from your man asking you to run a few of his errands so he can go to the gym after work—there goes your Pilates class, but you felt kind of guilty taking time for that anyway so, oh well!

If you have kids some compromise is a given but how much is too much? If by the end of the day you are exhausted that's a sign you are overly doing for others and need to find some balance.

Beth loved being a mom—to the point where her plans often got nixed if one of her kids asked her to do something for them. Whether she was on her way to a yoga class, to have lunch with a friend or pursue her love of singing, if her kids wanted her to do laundry or make them something to eat or take them shopping she would abandon her self-nurturing plans to satisfy their needs. Beth was so programmed to putting herself last, she didn't even see that her teenage kids were totally capable of doing for themselves. Like many women, the thought of breaking her pattern made her feel guilty. By compromising your needs you reinforce that you don't matter, and you end up feeling dull, robotic and lifeless.

After some deep digging Beth realized she was afraid of losing love if she put her needs first—even with her kids. Delving into her past and healing that core belief allowed her to live with more balance and honor her needs. That looked like letting her teenagers do their own laundry, clean their rooms and cook once in a while so she could take a run on the beach or meet a friend for dinner. These small things were huge and she realized by setting boundaries her kids actually ended up respecting her more.

People Pleasing

Katie's core need to be liked and approved of had her saying yes to every request that came her way. Her boss overloaded her with projects that weren't in her job description, her family had her running in circles on her off time, and her friends knew they could count on her for late night counseling when they couldn't sleep. Stretched way too thin Katie became full of resentment and her normally bubbly personality nearly flat-lined.

Many women like Katie please out of obligation, guilt or a similar need to be liked. It always backfires because when the motivation for giving isn't based in love it becomes laborious, a chore and a drain.

Another fast way to say goodbye to passion is to run yourself ragged on a regular basis, depriving you of joy. I've certainly fallen into this trap, haven't you? Said yes because that's what a "good" friend, wife, daughter, sister, employee would do, right? But what I discovered is "doing" for any reason other than pure service is a disservice to myself as well as the people in my life because I'm not authentically there for them and they can feel it. Even if I have a smile on my face my energy is saying, "I'm being put out" and the situation is charged with an unpleasant feeling.

Since everything is energy, double check your motivation before taking action and make sure you will be staying in your heart—otherwise you'll be spewing toxins into the airwaves. Ask yourself, "Am I helping to be of service? Will my action add joy and happiness or will it create another toxic dump site?"

On the other hand, if your good deeds are heart based it's a total win-win. There is no better feeling or way to refuel than when you are authentically in service.

Living Someone Else's Dreams

Have you ever thought about how you are living your life? Is it based on your desires and choices or someone else's? Let's start by looking at your career—is it a profession you chose or was it influenced by your parents, a favorite teacher or a friend you admired?

Jill wanted to be an artist but her father told her she would never make it and convinced her to choose a more stable profession. She followed his path and went into law, hating every minute of it. She didn't want to disappoint her dad, but every morning when her alarm went off she felt the life drain out of her body and she was filled with an overwhelming sense of dread.

When you give up your dreams to live someone else's you give up on that part of your soul that gives you the sparkle, the joy in life. In doing so you bury yourself a little more every day. When you aren't living your own life a deep-rooted anger starts to grow. Mostly, you're angry with yourself for abandoning YOU, but you may blind yourself to this truth and blame others instead to avoid taking responsibility for your life.

So many of the women I work with initially tell me they don't have any anger. It's not that they're being dishonest; they just don't give themselves permission to feel it or admit it. Again, it's the "good girls don't get angry" syndrome—it's epidemic! But you know what? Women *do* get angry and it's OK! When you don't honor your emotions your body will start talking to you, generally with illness. This is how you know you aren't living an authentic life.

So, acknowledge your anger. It doesn't mean you're a bad person or less deserving. It actually empowers you when you express it in a healthy way. I'm not saying to vent like a crazy person, hurting others in the process, but do find a way to get it out. Whether you get in your car or hop in the shower and scream at the top of your lungs—release! And take some time to reflect on why you are angry so that you can heal it. Over time as you release and heal you'll find you put yourself in situations less and less that create the anger.

Another prong to this ill-fated fork is that you'll end up losing respect for yourself. By not standing up for your big vision and setting boundaries, you are training others not to respect you too—another way you live small and dampen joy.

After Jill released her anger she came to a peaceful place where she was able to connect with her true feminine power and make the decision to quit law and pursue her artistry. She had such confidence and conviction about her choice her father respected her decision and stopped imposing his will on her.

Maintaining your passion for life has to do with how you interact with life every day and the choices that you make in every moment.

Stuffing Your Emotions

Emotions are neither good nor bad—they are just forms of energy. But we've been conditioned to believe that certain emotions like anger are bad and other emotions like love are good. If you are raised in a family environment where it's not OK to express what is considered to be a negative emotion, you'll sit with it or bury it rather than get it up and out in a healthy way. And what do you think starts to happen to that pure diamond essence within when you do this? It gets covered with dirty, grimy gunk. All of that impure energy becomes soot on your beautiful gemstone.

Imagine a fireplace and the soot that starts to cover the bricks.

Remember the toxicity of your emotions going out when you're not speaking from your heart? Well, now we have the same situation but it's imploding. It's polluting your body, your mind and your spirit. It takes a lot of energy to keep a lid on this emotion; over time it creates exhaustion and illness.

Dealing with Expectations

Expectations can get us into a heap of trouble. For example, when you get married you expect your partner to be loyal, honest and trustworthy. When you have kids you expect them to be healthy, well behaved and make a life they love. When you put your heart and soul into your job you expect to be appreciated and valued. When you eat well and exercise you expect to be healthy and trim. But the truth is, as you go through life you find out there are no guarantees. What you thought was a given could end up turning your world upside down.

Generally, when a woman's reality doesn't match her expectations, she starts to do a slow slide into disappointment and self-criticism thinking she must have done something wrong to create this unexpected twist of fate. Yes, we women are notorious for taking the blame, especially in relationships, beating ourselves up and dimming our beautiful essence in the process.

And when we are in this contracted state it's virtually impossible to have that open, expansive, love-filled life that we want. Now we've unwittingly created a life that's diametrically opposed to what we genuinely desire. So it's important to look at how we deal with the change-up when our expectations aren't being met.

Are you able to:

1) Reassess
2) Go with the flow
3) Regroup
4) Move forward

Or do you:

1) Shut down
2) Contract
3) Withdraw
4) Isolate

When I got married I expected my husband to be faithful. We discussed infidelity before we got married and he promised to let me know if his testosterone had urges to surge elsewhere. So when I discovered he was having an affair it was jolting. My shock absorbers were not prepared for this speed bump. I went back and forth blaming him, then me, then him, then me. I felt betrayed, confused, angry, sad and lost. After the big tears stopped, I realized I could never trust him again, owned my part, accepted that my life would never be the same and began to regroup. Dealing with unmet expectations can be a slip and slide for sure, but moving forward with a good plan and mindset will give you traction.

Part of the slip and slide for women are the insecurities that crop up when our expectations go south. We are tempted to listen to all the cruel chatter that runs incessantly through our minds—you're not pretty enough, smart enough, thin enough, sexy enough, good enough. Or maybe you bought into the belief that you aren't a good mother, wife, daughter, sister, friend or employee. *Ay yi yi*, it can drive you crazy!

Part of my healing journey included yoga. During one practice my instructor gave us a profound fact: the average person has 60,000 – 80,000 thoughts per day and of these more than 80% are negative! That hit me like a ton of bricks. No wonder we can nosedive into a downward spiral if we don't put the brakes on our thoughts. That invalidating self-talk has got to go! It's time to become your biggest fan and staunchest supporter.

Comparing Yourself to Others

Then there's the trap of comparing yourself to other women, especially if you grew up competing with your sisters for your parents' approval and love. Or if your partner has a wandering eye you may find yourself asking, "What does *she* have that I don't?"

If you look at other women as competition instead of a loving sisterhood you are robbing yourself of a supportive community. Comparing can be a double-edged sword—you're either going to feel like you don't measure up or you are going to feed your ego and give yourself a false sense of importance. Either side is dangerous for your well-being.

Did you know your insecurities create an energetic message that screams to the world you are not enough? It's like a megaphone projecting your inner thoughts and they can be heard either as arrogance or weakness. Neither is what you want the world to be hearing!

What you really want is connection but your insecurities are creating separation. And you will never get the respect you desire with either attitude. The best way to overcome insecurities and build confidence is to take positive action steps like the ones you'll be learning with the SPARKLE System.

Communication Breakdown

Communication is another slippery slope. That old saying, "You get more with honey than vinegar" couldn't be more accurate. There have been several studies corroborating that 93% of communication effectiveness is determined by nonverbal cues. That's right, only 7% of your communication is based on what you say—55% is your body language and 38% is your tone.

So take a moment and think about your communication style? Is your voice like velvet or are your words like fingernails on a chalkboard? Are you demanding, demeaning or bossy? Good relationships require respectful communication.

If you grew up in a home like I did, where your expressed emotions were not welcomed or acknowledged with respect, as an adult you may be hesitant to share your feelings or they may come out in an immature, volatile tirade. If this is you, challenge yourself to grow and evolve by standing up for yourself and communicate like an adult without blame, criticism or judgment when someone crosses your boundaries. When you overcome the fear of losing love, being disapproved of or blowing the relationship, you'll find the opposite actually happens. The irony is that when you express your thoughts and needs with confidence and maturity, you'll gain respect from the other person.

Understanding What Makes Men Tick

Let's look at an important caveat. Even when you do successfully express yourself, what about understanding the communication differences between men and women? Women tend to focus on how to create a solution that works for everyone, talking through issues, and paying attention to nonverbal cues such as tone, emotion, and empathy. Men are more task-oriented, tend to be less talkative, and are more isolated. Men have a hard time understanding emotions that aren't explicitly laid out compared to women who have the ability to intuit feelings and subtle cues.

The male and female brains are quite different as well. Whereas men are more left brained and solution oriented, women can process equally well between both hemispheres. This means when you are trying to solve a problem he wants to take action and you are more creative and aware of feelings wanting to talk things through to resolve a situation.

When you ask your partner for his advice he'll expect you to listen without interrupting and run with his wisdom. Take this tip and you'll win the gold! To keep a man feeling brawny, honor his thoughts and perspectives, appreciate his help and make him feel like your hero. When you make a man feel like your hero he will go to the ends of the earth for you; criticize him and he'll run for the hills.

Your life will be much easier when you understand and honor the following needs of your man:

1) He needs to feel needed.
2) He wants to be your hero.
3) He wants to fix your problems.
4) He wants to be appreciated.
5) He needs to feel he can win with you.

You can see how the disconnect happens if you have a tendency to be independent. It's really so simple—when a man feels good about himself when he's with you he'll treat *you* like a queen. Promise. So let him know how much you appreciate him and his heroic help. If you have resistance to this, look at it this way: you want a different result, right? So don't get frustrated, get smart. You are a brilliant and savvy woman; start engaging with men in a way that will bring you the delicious relationship you desire.

Think about it—would you continue to go to an empty well expecting to get water when you know it's dry? It's no different with men. True, they are wired differently, but why not understand this and honor it! Open to a new approach and stay focused on your long-term goal...love, connection, intimacy...and you'll have a win-win result.

Living in Your Masculine Energy

Are you Clark Kent to the rescue? Do you fly around looking for ways to save the day? Are you so independent, capable and strong it makes a man feel like he has nothing of value to offer? Many very accomplished and competent women often complain they intimidate men. If you have been told this it most likely means you are in your masculine energy. And it would be more true to say when a man is in your space he doesn't feel needed. When a man doesn't feel needed he will shut down or go where he *is* needed.

Balancing the male and female energies is a beautiful dance. Every person has both and will design a much happier life when they are able to successfully discern when it's appropriate to "do" and when it's better just to "be."

How we choose to use our energy is about our approach to life. We all have a strategy to get what we want, and we have been taught how to get what we want from our parents and siblings. My mom was the primary person in my life growing up. She was strong, giving, competent, tireless, controlling and independent. She stuffed a lot of her emotions but I always felt anger in her silence. Without a doubt, she wore the pants in the family. The message I got was that men are never around to help and when they are they are pretty much useless. Needless to say, my ex was the poster boy for this belief. Since my divorce I've taken the time to develop familial and platonic relationships with men who are helpful and "take charge" types to help me reprogram this inaccurate assumption.

Did you know before you turned six you were predominantly in Delta or Theta brain wave states, the states hypnotherapists drop their clients into in order to make them more suggestible? This explains why children take on the beliefs, attitudes and behaviors of the adults around them as truths. If this programming isn't challenged or reprogrammed then these "truths" become the default patterns of how we live and create results. If you operate more in your masculine your partner will be more in his feminine. After understanding this it was pretty easy to see how my programming created my circumstances and the type of men I attracted.

If you are single you may have no choice but to step into the masculine role to handle day-to-day needs. But getting used to doing things on your own can be a double-edged sword—it's necessary but after a while if you start owning those masculine traits, you will forget what it feels like to be in your feminine.

How about honoring yourself for being capable but always keep the vision front and center of what it would feel like to have a man do the manly things for you so you'll be able to flip to feminine when appropriate? This way when a man offers you'll be comfortable letting him take over rather than blocking his help with a reactive, "I got it."

Some of you may be so steeped in the masculine you don't even know it, so let's take a look at typical masculine and feminine traits.

Masculine: aggressive, logical, leading, directive, decisive, protecting, providing, competitive, planning, strong, vying for power, controlling.

Feminine: intuitive, connective, relatedness, receiving, cooperation, emotional, collaborative, bonding, flowing, magnetic.

How are you running your energy?

Lovers or Roommates?

Even if you are in a relationship you may feel lonely, depressed and disconnected. Sadly, many couples live like roommates instead of caring, passionate partners and lovers. The reality hits when you wake up one morning, look over at your partner and feel nothing but friendship or worse yet, disconnection. Of course this estrangement doesn't happen overnight although it may feel like it...you wonder, "*How* did we get to this place?"

The truth is there's no one answer; it's a million little things that have become one BIG thing. Therein lies the blindness—a little upset here, a little letdown there doesn't seem like a problem—and if you communicate and resolve things as they come up it's not. But most of us want to blind ourselves to the truth so we sweep everything unpleasant under the carpet. Over time your feelings become buried so deep you disconnect, numb out, become robotic and lose your passion to the point you have no clue how to get back to what was...so you grow farther and farther apart.

You realize there is no excitement in your relationship, or

your life. When you catch a glimpse of your reflection there's no twinkle in your eye, no rosiness in your cheeks, no smile on your face. Wow, what a wake-up call! This doesn't match the vision you had for yourself!

You need to recapture that vivacious woman you once were...and that comes from the inside...that sparkle, that zest for life, that joie de vivre—it comes from the inside out.

Polishing Your Diamond Power

Not surprisingly, when any or all of these patterns insidiously infuse your life, you begin to notice your sparkle fading and your reflection becoming unfamiliar. The worst thing is you have no idea how to get your glow back. All the things you want in your life—the deeply loving connection, passion, intimacy and happiness—are being blocked.

The good news is the journey back starts with you—you have total control.

The great secret to satisfying those longings of the soul is reconnecting to your diamond power—the God-given radiance you were born with, the authentic core of who you are. And when you connect with this essence you will be reminded, no matter what your beliefs may be, that you are whole and perfect. Connect to this energy in prayer or meditation, and when you fill up with peace and love, own it with pride. Every person is a unique incarnation of God with a special gift. You have a purpose in just "being"—you don't have to "do" anything. This alignment will dismantle your fears and insecurities, balance your energies, and fill you up with so much joy and gratitude enabling you to fall hopelessly in love with YOU so you can start living the life you've always wanted.

The quickest way to reconnect with your diamond power is by using the SPARKLE System outlined in this book. The beauty of this system is that it can be implemented and used over and over again. If you are like me, you'll find your life is a series of highs and lows; it's easy to keep your sparkle when things are going well. But what about when a challenge presents and you latch onto an old way of thinking or acting and the sparkle flies out the window? You better believe this is going to happen; it's a reality.

For a long time I felt like a fraud, teaching people how to get their sparkle on when I couldn't keep my own shining brightly 100% of the time. I discovered I had a perfection thread operating; the truth is *no one* is sparkling 24/7—it's impossible. What is possible, however, is having a system in place that helps you regroup and gives you the tools to lead yourself out of tough situations and unhappy moods so that your brilliance will rise again.

This is the key—understanding you will go in and out of feeling fabulous and that's OK. The important thing is that you make the choice to use the SPARKLE System every time you feel lost and disempowered so that you make the most of your precious time on this planet.

Before I unveil the SPARKLE System please take some time to honestly look at your life as it is today and identify what is blocking your bliss. Then make a commitment to leave it behind. This will catapult your transformation.

The fastest way to get to the most magnificent version of you is honesty, so take your time and answer the questions below with as much candor as possible—and remember, no one will see them but you.

Pause and Reflect

1) Make a list of your *radiance robbers,* choose one and take an action step every day for one week to create a new positive pattern. Rinse and repeat.

2) What is your pay-off for your belief patterns? For example, if you find yourself in situations where you are always "the victim" what do you get out of this? Attention? Separation? Get to blame others so you don't have to take responsibility for your actions? Stay small so you don't have to shine your light big and bright? What new behaviors can you take to step out of this pattern and stand in your power?

3) Set new boundaries this week by saying no to a request you don't want to do.

Revel in Your Radiance

When I was going through my divorce and self-absorbed with its challenges, a dear friend told me the quickest way to feel good was to do something nice for someone else. So I went and got a beautiful card, enclosed a letter of deep gratitude and sent it to a girlfriend who had been a huge support. All of my stress vanished and my heart felt warm and expanded as soon as I sent it off. I have never forgotten this simple yet sage advice and still practice it today. I invite you to think of a service you can do for others to gracefully lead yourself out of a funk.

CHAPTER 3

Soul Sister Support

Where would we be without our core group of girlfriends? They love you, laugh with you, and stand by your side when facing fears and upsets. Your true friends will set you straight when you're going 'round the bend, bring you chocolate when you're down, and pour the champagne when you're on fire. They want the best for you, *always.*

Since the beginning of time women have bonded and formed community to inspire, motivate, and help each other overcome and thrive. Even if you're in a relationship and your man is your best friend, you still need your gal pals. Why? Simply, men are wired differently. They want to fix. We want to vent before looking for a solution—driving a guy crazy. It's not fair to expect men to always be there for our emotional needs. Most of them do their best, God love 'em, but generally they can only listen for "so long" before they need to slip away to recharge their testosterone.

A great gift of friendship is the phenomenal *support* our sisterhood generously gives us. Who else can you share your secrets with and trust they'll take them to their grave? Who else can you bounce an idea off of and have them just listen and explore it with you without getting pissy if you don't take their advice? (You *know* what I'm talking about!) And what about when life seems hard and unfair, and starts spinning out of control with stresses, challenges and responsibilities? It's your friends who help you let it all go and bring back a sense of balance. They give you perspective and peace, reminding you of who you are and what's really important. And, they make you laugh.

This chapter celebrates the magic and wonder of female friendship. The SPARKLE System and the Romance-Capades will move you out of your comfort zone and into your diamond essence. That's thrilling—but it can be scary, too. Make your process easy and fun by inviting your girlfriends along for the journey. Imagine how your Goddess self will soar with your friends cheering you on—and they'll grow into their own divahood at the same time. My circle of angels was key to my transformation. Let your friends be a key to yours too.

Girls Just Wanna Have Fun

There isn't a woman across the globe whose face doesn't light up with a huge smile and a mischievous glint in her eye when Cyndi Lauper's famous song, "Girls Just Wanna Have Fun," cranks through the airwaves. Open arm camaraderie, bonding, singing, dancing, and a lifetime of reminiscing are inspired all at once. You suddenly see yourself on a road trip with your favorite friends cruising in a sexy red convertible with the top down, singing at the top of your lungs with the music blaring—very *Thelma and Louise*. There may even be a Brad Pitt in the picture!

Most definitely, every adventure is made more fun with your soul sisters by your side to share the experience and give you the courage to step outside your comfort zone and try new things. They give you a chance to shed your role of mom, wife, daughter, sister and just be YOU!

Hey, our men are great but most of them don't have the emotional *oomph* of our gal pals. And last time I checked, most guys don't want to rush off with us to the nearest make-up counter to try the latest shade of lipstick, or get their nails done, or rummage through sale racks for a sexy frock. And they surely don't want to sit around and share feelings about life's journey, dissect conversations, process family dynamics or chitchat about nothing. Thank goodness our girlfriends want to do all these things—and more.

One of my most treasured memories is of a Valentine pamper-fest with my dear friends Patti and Maureen. Since my heart was healing and their husbands were both out of town we decided to spend this day of love together and enjoy it to the max. This brought a beautiful realization to the surface for both Patti and Maureen. Even though it wasn't possible to spend V-Day with their significant others, love isn't specific to the romantic rapture you have with your hubby or sweetheart—it includes girlfriends too. The love of friends is just as important as the love in an intimate relationship.

We gathered at my house and headed out for our first stop: a day spa for some serious spoiling. What fun we had lounging around after our treatments, gabbing in big comfy robes, getting the giggles and feeling like princesses. In a blissful mood we next wandered across the street to a beachside resort that made us feel like we were vacationing at a rich uncle's villa. As we sat leisurely taking in the vast ocean view, drinking Bloody Marys and eating the best eggs Benedict ever, we shared our thoughts and feelings on love and life, but most of all we laughed and laughed and laughed.

After that we went back to my house, popped some champagne, opened a box of Mary See's nuts and chews, and huddled together on my bed to watch the hauntingly beautiful and romantic movie, *Somewhere in Time*. You have to admit, watching a movie like this with your favorite friends is much different than seeing it with a guy. We smiled, sighed and cried together, feeling the joy and pain of Jane Seymour's character as if it were our own, creating another bond between us.

Inspired by the deep love depicted in the movie, Patti decided she wanted to plan a Romance-Capade for her man as a belated Valentine surprise. We were on it! Ideas flew, laughter filled the room, and within a short time the sultry Love Lounge singer was born. (See page 254.)

As we hugged goodbye we felt happiness for all that we had shared and also sadness that the day was over. There was also gratitude for the gift of our friendship, knowing our lives were brighter because of each other.

Soul Sisters Remind You of Your Magnificence

Sometimes along the road to becoming an adult you lose the ability to be yourself, worrying that you won't be accepted. You bury things deeply, fearful of judgment, and forget that you are this beautiful diamond. This is why you need your soul sisters:

to remind you of your magnificence, to inspire, support, and uplift you. They see you as you are now, without pigeonholing you as you were as a child. They see past the labels you've been given over the years; they see *you*. There is no threat or fear you'll be exposed—oh no, girlfriends are that safe haven that allows you to spread your wings, become the butterfly, and bust out of the cocoon, free to be YOU.

During and after my divorce I was blessed with an amazing group of friends I will always consider my special angels. We worked, traveled, shopped, laughed, cried, explored, and had a ball together. They were my biggest supporters. It was a vulnerable and raw time for me and they provided a safe net for me to free fall daily, grow and transform. Through this bonding we all became comfortable sharing our unique perspectives on life and love, letting go of inhibitions, openly expressing our deepest desires and fears. We became each other's greatest cheerleaders and sources of support and inspiration.

It was a sacred time together. For those few hours we gathered each day we didn't have to edit ourselves or wonder, "Is this politically correct? Will I be judged? What will they think of me if I reveal this or that?" We felt safe to expose the true person inside and knew there wouldn't be any dire consequences to our discussions. It was fun and freeing to be able to talk about everything from our wildest dreams to our biggest insecurities. Our cherished sisterhood provided an outlet where we gave each other the opportunity to be real, heal and shine. We gave ourselves permission to drop the masks.

Despite the circumstances of my divorce, my friends and I never sat around man-bashing or engaged in embitterment. To the contrary, since I was entering the dating world and Patti and Maureen were nurturing new marriages, we talked a lot about what makes a woman sensual and desirable and happy. While I was trying to find my femininity again—ditching the man boot to don the stiletto (both figuratively and literally)—Patti was focusing on what it meant to be married, how to balance being a wife with work and connecting with her femininity, as well as what it takes to make a relationship fresh, exciting and lasting. Maureen was trying to figure out how to talk about her desires within her marriage. This brought an interesting conversation to light: how to communicate about sexual desire within a relationship without feeling like a floozy.

It's shocking how many committed women are plagued with the good girl syndrome, afraid their partners and friends will see them as tramps if they admit to their lusty side. And heaven forbid they have more of a thirst than their mate! What would *that* say about them? As my friends revealed and later, many of my clients, certain cultures and religions have made women feel shameful about their desires, causing them to suppress and hide natural needs. Having an outlet where you feel safe to express these passions, and know there is nothing wrong with you, is invaluable.

It was the girlfriend lunches and get-togethers that helped me come to know myself again after my divorce. All of my friendships were a special blessing but there was something about the connection between Patti, Maureen and me that was magical, much like the *Sex and the City* sisterhood. Perhaps it was because we worked together and were a part of each other's daily life; perhaps it was because as I was divorcing they were marrying and wanted to learn what not to do. All I know is that it was as though we were pieces of a puzzle, giving and receiving exactly what the friendship needed for a perfect fit.

You can't have this with everyone. My friends and I found a place to have a happy spot. Everyone has that place inside, but we found a way to bring that happy place out and bring it to each other. This is the magic you can also create.

Friendship Fairy Dust

Your truest of friends sprinkle healing fairy dust when times are tough. They are there to listen, give you a shoulder to cry on, and a big gooey brownie with triple fudge frosting to get you through your trying times.

I will never forget the time I walked into my ob-gyn's office for a routine visit and found the waiting room full of waddling women ready to deliver. Forty-ish, I felt a wave of reality roll through my body—that would *never* be me. Neither married nor engaged, with no boyfriend in sight, my chances of having a child were slim to none. My window for giving birth was pretty much over. Somehow I held it together for my appointment, but as soon as I got in my car the tears spilled over. I sobbed the whole way home for the child I would never have. Even if I met the man of my dreams the very next day, I could not see myself having the energy to raise a child into my 60s. I had thought about this and accepted it intellectually, but until that day I had never stared it in the face and felt the pain so deeply in my soul.

I would never know the joy of holding my own sweet baby and feel that unconditional love so many mothers speak of. My friends held the space for me to grieve, never trying to "fix" me or find a solution. They just let me feel the deep-seated sorrow. Their love and support was a generous gift I will always be grateful for—a true blessing.

After that I realized that God had a different plan for me. That's when I began to see even more clearly that my purpose is to teach other women what I have learned and continue to overcome along my journey.

Girlfriends Get It

You share differently with your friends than you do your partner because women have an inherent understanding of what you are going through. You can get yourself so riled up you think whatever's rocking your world is just happening to you, but it's not.

As women we are all going through similar emotional challenges—marriages falling apart, problems with our kids, health issues, aging parents, job loss or change, hormones disappearing, weight appearing. It's one thing to go through it on your own and another to have a friend to call and say, "Wow, am I having a day." Girlfriends restore your balance when you feel like you're on a tilt-a-whirl. They don't look at you with a blank stare when you're having a meltdown—they get it!

Friends validate that you are not alone, crazy or paranoid. They are there to live, laugh and love with you, providing the type of therapy no amount of money can buy because it's all wrapped in loving care. As a matter of fact research now tells us friendships are even more critical to our health and well-being than family relationships. They will always be there for you and you'll always be there for them. At the end of the day, your friends are there for everything.

And what about aging? We're not going to change getting gray hair, sprouting nose hair (ugh, how did *that* happen?!), losing skin tone, and dealing with muffin tops, varicose veins, moles, wrinkles, sagging breasts, dimpled derrieres—need I go on? Fortunately, we are all in this together. There's no escaping aging so at least we can laugh about it—together.

Keep the Connection

Aren't old friends the best? It's like putting on your favorite bathrobe—warm and cozy without any pretense. They know you inside and out and wrap you in love regardless. I don't know about you, but I thank God for the pinky-swear pact my friends and I made years ago to stay a part of each other's lives, no matter what challenges and changes transpired.

Have you kept up your connection with your female posse? Do you make it a practice to get together on a regular basis? If so, *fannntassstic*. But if you've let them slide, think about *why*. Are you a workaholic, an accomplishment junkie? Are you depressed, stressed out? Perhaps you've let your partner be your everything and lost track of friends. When life's challenges hit you will feel very alone if you have not maintained your friendships. Letting your friends go is a big mistake; it creates a huge hole in your heart.

Take a minute to think about how you can better balance your time to include your friends. Make it a point to reconnect. Don't wait! It's not hard to be a good friend—and it needn't take much time if your schedule is tight.

Here are a few fun ideas for girly get-togethers:

- Cocktail Soiree—Invite your girlfriends over for a cocktail party. Welcome them with some divine diva tunes. (Sister Sledge's "We are Family" is always a crowd pleaser!) Set out some simple appetizers and set up a cocktail corner with some marvelous pink martinis. As the night gets rolling you might want to clear those tabletops because if your friends are anything like mine, some sexy, sassy dancing is sure to start!

- Pamper Party—Gather your soul sisters for an evening of spa sensations. Tell them all to bring comfy robes and slippers and their drink of desire. Bring in a massage therapist and a manicurist. Spoil yourselves silly!
- Movie Magic—Invite a friend over and either treat yourselves to an endless night of eye-candy watching your favorite heartthrob or make it a chick flick night.
- Annual Get-together—Once you're happily hooked up it's not always easy to see friends as often as it was when you were single. But if you make it a priority you can still keep the bond strong through some sort of annual event. Several years ago one of my dearest friends and I started a tradition of kicking off the Christmas season with a holiday walk down Montana Avenue in Santa Monica. Sometimes other friends join us, making it all the merrier, but if no one else can come we know we can count on each other because it's our tradition and we are committed! We stroll down the street listening to carolers, drinking champagne, laughing and being silly as we hop in and out of the beautifully decorated stores. It's one of the highlights of my year. The beauty of such a good friend is that no matter how long it's been since we've seen each other, we pick up right where we left off and have a blast together.

Girlfriend connection is always a hot topic for my angel circle. We all agree how important it is to *stay connected,* how necessary it is to get a break and taste a smidgeon of the carefree life we had before family responsibilities became the priority. It's a part of being feminine—women need other women. *Women make each other feel fabulous. Women help each other BECOME better women.*

Create Your Own Sisterhood

Whether you're single or coupled up life is always more enjoyable when you have a friend or two by your side. Why not create your own "Sexy & Sparkling After 40" group? Get them involved in your journey—and help spark theirs. Gift them with this book and make this a fun adventure you do together. Keeping each other accountable will help you step out of a life you no longer enjoy to create a life you'll love. Hold a dazzling vision for each other, encourage those actions that may seem scary, collaborate and share ideas, ultimately supporting the dreams and desires each of you craves.

If you're attached you can help each other plan Romance-Capades that will ignite your love life and make you feel alive and flushed with sensuality. If you're single, play with the Romance-Capades to magnetize the love of your dreams. You can rehearse until the real thing sweeps you off your feet!

Why not form your own romantic rendezvous clique—an exclusive, enviable group of women who choose to brainstorm ways to add romance, passion and love to relationship rather than sit around and complain, focusing on what's lacking? Be a trendsetter and master this art! Wouldn't you be proud to be a pioneer of such a positive trend?

Now that you've gotten clear on what's been dimming your dazzle, and you're spending time with your girlfriends, you're set to explore the first step of the SPARKLE System. It's all about seeing your glorious future.

Pause and Reflect

1) If you've never had really close friends or have moved and want to make new friends, ask yourself "What qualities do I want in a friend?" Make a list and then become those yourself—you have to be a good friend before you will attract good friends.

2) Join a club or take a class in something that interests you. This is a great way to meet like-minded women. Not only will stepping into that feminine space of friendship help you connect to your own feminine power, research proves that women with a wide social network have higher self-esteem and less stress, live longer, and are happier and healthier.

Revel in Your Radiance

Take a moment and give a silent prayer of thanks for each and every one of your friends. Then let them know what a difference they've made in your life by sending them a card, giving them a call, or sending a heartfelt email or text. Make their day, as they've so often made yours, by letting them know how grateful you are for their love, laughter and support. Friends are definitely the joy of life!

Chapter 4

S…See Your Bright Future

Do you have a clear vision of your future? Could you describe it in detail right now or is it a little fuzzy? Maybe you see bits and pieces or perhaps you don't see anything but a big black void. Regardless, know that you can have the magical, love-filled life you desire. All you have to do is get crystal clear about what you want and stay connected to that vision every day.

If you don't know what you want it will be reflected in your present circumstances. If your future is fuzzy or non-existent, you probably are experiencing a life without direction and it may feel a lot like the movie *Groundhog Day*. You may feel stuck or stagnant, unhappy, disappointed and disillusioned.

Has your life turned out the way you thought it would? If not, are you focusing all your energy on what went wrong or are you creating a brilliant, bright future? Most people want a future that's warm and fuzzy and filled with fulfillment. Yet we go through life blaming our circumstances for the life we have, not realizing we are responsible for co-creating our future with our thoughts and words. Whether we are stuck in the past, seeing nothing at all ahead, or envisioning a dazzling future—all are equal in producing our reality.

My friend Ti Caine, Future Visioning Expert, expanded my awareness of how critical clarity is for a happy life. If we are dissatisfied yet do nothing to change, we will continue to live a mediocre existence at best. And then wonder what happened to that fabulous life we dreamed of having as a child. When you were a kid and someone asked you what life would look like as an adult, didn't it seem like nothing was too great to achieve? Weren't you riding a rocket straight to the moon?

But sadly for most, adulthood saw only a handful of our dreams materialize. Various life experiences pulled you off track and created distraction. Without a clear vision, obstacles and challenges can feel like failures and wipe out your enthusiasm. Eventually you may give up—thinking it's too late and you get what you get. Maybe your desires are so buried you've forgotten how to dream and you've accepted a blah existence.

Here's the good news—you always have choice! And when you give yourself permission to dream again, becoming clear about what it would be like to have what you want in your life, you are powerfully co-creating a juicy and delicious life! See your diamond bright future and bring it powerfully into manifestation—the first step in the SPARKLE System.

Are You on Auto-Pilot?

Who—or what—is steering your life? Are you in the driver's seat or have you defaulted to programming? Take a few moments to do the following exercise and you'll see the profound difference between knowing and choosing where you are going and not knowing.

Close your eyes and imagine you are walking down a dark alley. It's nighttime, and you can't see very well because it's foggy and pouring rain. The alley is narrow, smelly, unfamiliar and full of shadows; you aren't sure what's up ahead. Notice what you are feeling. What is happening in your body? Do you have a pit in your stomach? Are you anxious and agitated? Where do you feel this in your body? Are you contracted, fearful? If there was someone next to you telling a story would you be able to give your full attention? Isn't it impossible to concentrate when you have so much anxiety? If you had to spend six months, six years or the rest of your life walking down this alley, how would you feel? Probably pretty miserable, right?

Sadly, a large percent of the population has been programmed for this dark future, which creates anxiety, wears you down, and causes aging. Not surprising, it's difficult to connect in a loving way when you are experiencing this level of fear.

Okay, now shake it off knowing you can make a different choice. Take a few deep breaths and center yourself.

Close your eyes again, but this time, imagine you are in a beautiful future. You're walking on a gorgeous glittering path of diamonds overlooking the ocean; it's a bright sunny day and the landscape around you is absolutely magnificent, fragrant with lush flowers. The sky is crystal blue with billowing white clouds and since there aren't any people around, you can walk as fast or leisurely as you want. Out over the horizon is a wonderful experience and although you can't see it yet you know whatever you are headed for is going to be joyful, fun and fulfilling. How do you feel? What's happening in your body? Is your heart opening? Do you feel happy, hopeful, excited and expansive?

Take a deep breath into that expansion and fullness. It's subtle so pay attention to it and allow yourself to feel it fully. Now, if this were your future how would you feel? Present, courageous, confident? Maybe even sassy? If someone were walking next to you and wanted to talk would you be able to fully focus on the conversation? Being in the "now" is natural when you are relaxed and happy.

Think about this for a moment, you get to create your future! As a matter of fact, if you don't you will default to childhood programming, largely influenced by your parents, and that will determine your destiny. Take a look at your current circumstances, you will see many aspects of your life reflect what you or other people told you you could have—they are consistent with your identity and how you see yourself.

Think about your parents. Have you followed in their footsteps? Developing the same health problems, divorcing or suffering through an unhappy marriage, career choices, lifestyle, financial gains or struggles, feeling victimized or stuck? It's not unusual to have the expectation that the same life awaits you. If you don't consciously replace this expectation with what *you* choose, your life will run on auto-pilot.

If you want to go to New York you don't head towards Los Angeles, do you? Absolutely not, you *see yourself* in New York and then you fill in the details—how long you'll stay, where you'll stay, what you'll do, how you'll get there. You start researching the city, sifting through all the fabulous activity options so that you make the most of your time. You find out what you'll need, what the weather will be like so you can pack the perfect outfits and how much money your visit will cost. And then, if you decide to drive, you get in your car, consult your map, and head towards the Big Apple. If you get a flat tire, you fix it, get back on the road and continue towards New York. No matter what obstacle presents on the trip, you are clear about your destination and unruffled.

The same goes for any and all aspects of your future.

The Whole Enchilada

What do you *really* want? For those of you who are clear about your future, kudos! For those of you who aren't, ask yourself this question, "What would my life look like if I were living as an empowered sparkling sexy woman?"

Would you have a deeply connected and passionate relationship with that hunky man of your dreams? How about letting that ultra-sensual fit and healthy body come out to play? Then there's that incredibly exciting career that's not only fulfilling but catapults you out of bed every morning with unbridled enthusiasm for the day. Is your bank account big and fat allowing you to have that magnificent Mediterranean home overlooking the ocean?

Determine what you want, write it down, talk about it, imagine you already have it, and watch it become your reality. Can you see how getting clear will bring you your bliss? Sometimes we attract less than ideal circumstances because we're not sure about our own desires. Getting crystal clear is key! Every aspect of your life is interrelated, so if you want change look at the following ten areas of your life and give yourself permission to envision what each category would look like if it were a 10. Answer the questions as your future Self.

1) Health and body—Do you have a nutritious diet? Are you happy with your body weight? How do you take care of yourself?
2) Relationship—Describe the details of your perfect partner and relationship together.
3) Finance—How much money do you make? How much do you have in savings and investments?
4) Career—What are you doing? How many days a week do you work?
5) Emotional—What is your general disposition? How do you handle challenge?
6) Femininty/Sensuality—Describe your essence, how you feel within, how you interact with others.
7) Social— Do you have positive, like-minded friends who support your needs?
8) Spiritual—What is your relationship with God/Divine/Source?
9) Making a Difference—how do you contribute to others and the world?
10) Free Time/Fun Life Experiences—What brings you joy?

What else do you want? The sky's the limit! Think of every aspect of your life. Remember you can have it ALL—as far and wide and technicolored as your imagination can fathom. So give yourself permission to dream...BIG! Get as detailed as possible. The more specific you are the easier it will be to bring forth your vision.

How do you feel right now? Thrilled? Anxious? Expansive? Excited? Scared? Inspired? Hopeful? Doubtful? Take some deep relaxing breaths and let yourself percolate. Let it sink in that you have control over the course of your life. If you have felt like a buoy in the ocean bobbing about at the mercy of the waves, you now know you can anchor yourself with a clear vision of your choice. (If some parts of the vision are still fuzzy, no worries. The next chapter, Pinpoint Your Passions, will help you reconnect with what gives you joy. From there it will be easy to decide what you want!)

Acting "As If"

When you intentionally co-create your future you have the opportunity to shift your perception of who you are. Say you are single, independent and used to being alone but you want a deeply loving relationship. There is a huge gap in the way you are living and the life you want. To close the gap you will need to switch out the identity of being alone with an identity of being in a relationship—you'll need to act "as if" you're already living the delicious future of your dreams. See it, feel it, taste it!

To begin a seismic shake-up start imagining yourself with an engagement ring on your finger. Notice how it feels. How happy are you? Can you feel your fiancé's hand in yours? What are your senses saying? Take this experience to the core of your being. Ground it into your foundational make-up.

Samantha, had been with her boyfriend for 12 years and desperately wanted to marry him. However, he was not the marrying kind and was satisfied with the way things were. In her heart she knew this was the man she was meant to be with. So she started envisioning their wedding day—she saw herself walking down the aisle and felt the tingles of happiness. Samantha clearly envisioned him waiting for her with a big smile as well as many other details. The entire scene was always illuminated in gold light and ultimately became a knowing for her. Her ability to see and feel what she wanted, taking it into the fiber of her being brought this dream to reality. She's been happily married for over 10 years now.

Another example, Susan, was in love with a man who was a bit of a marriage-phobe, but she also dreamed of making her relationship official. So every day on her hour-long commute to work she imagined she had a beautiful big engagement ring on her finger. As the sun shone through the windshield she envisioned her diamond sparkling so much it was blinding. As she envisioned the ring she deeply felt what it would be like to actually have it on her finger and move through her day. She also imagined what it would be like to hold her lover's hand as his fiancée. Within a year of doing this she was engaged!

Both of these stories are great examples of the power of clarity and staying focused on the end result. I'm sure both these women had challenging times while in their relationships but they stayed focused on their dream. They also relied on their strong faith, trusting the door would close if their desires were not in their best interest. They allowed themselves to have the vision but to stay open to the flow, without forcing.

When you want to create a future that's outside your current reality you have to consistently act "as if" you are already that person with the life you desire in a very solid way. Feel it in your body! Strongly! Get outrageously detailed about the ways you will change your life to match the future you are committed to creating. To manifest your desires and goals follow these steps:

1) Determine new behavioral patterns to adopt to support your desires.

2) Decide how you want to present to others.
3) Choose how you will spend your time.
4) Create a vision board using photos and words reflecting your desires.
5) When you look at each photo on the board say, "I'm so grateful to have this in my life now! This is who I am!"

These will all help you shift to attain your desired future. What new actions and routines will you put in place? Will you join an activity club or meet-up group, take a new class, read books that will help you with your mindset, spend time with loving couples who model what you want, make time for fun? Are you committed to changing and diving into delicious?

At the same time you'll need to ground your visioning on a regular basis. To get the results you want it is important to be as specific as possible, as consistently as possible. So when you are imagining you're dancing under the moonlight with your perfect partner, envision the setting. What are you wearing? How you are feeling? What is he whispering in your ear? Is there a scent in the air? Can you feel the night air on your skin?

Connecting to your senses, particularly audio, visual, and kinesthetic, will enable you to embody the new you that much faster. Remember, as you are imagining, you are feeling it deeply in your body. The most important thing to get is WHO ARE YOU and WHO DO YOU WANT TO BE in this life? See your sparkling Self gracing the world, your vivacious vixen unleashing, your sensuality soaring!

Inner and Outer Harmony

To receive this glorious future you are co-creating, you also need to focus on your inner development. Do you need to become more vulnerable, seeing it as a strength instead of a weakness? Do you need to open your heart more so you can give and receive the flow of love? How is your self-esteem—are you comfortable speaking up, expressing your thoughts and setting boundaries? Do you communicate from your heart without judgment, blame or manipulation? Are you able to share your feelings with transparency? What steps will you take to evolve and grow your inner game? What support will you need to succeed?

You can make this process of self-reflection fun and simple. But don't forget, your current identity didn't form overnight, dear heart. Be patient with unearthing your beautiful and brilliant sparkle. Anchor into a strong belief in your vision, stay consistent, and you will clear the crud and allow your magnificence to shine!

Let me tell you, I've been there. The year I was going through my divorce was such an emotionally difficult time for me, but it was also one of the most exciting times of my life. I had the opportunity to re-create "me." It started with the honest talk I had with my friend Jon—finding out how I presented, taking it in, and then deciding how I wanted to show up in the world. That started the wheels turning. The next thing I knew I was thumbing through magazines and found the "me" I wanted to become in the Manolo Blahnik sparkling stiletto.

That page was posted to my bulletin board in my office and every time I looked at it I saw myself as a vibrant, happy, sensual and vivacious woman. I also saw myself in love with life *and* a wonderful man. Through the grace of God and the vibration of my thoughts, things started to shift, shake and shimmer for me. I changed my hair and make-up, bought a sexy new wardrobe, took tons of fun girl trips from Hawaii to Paris and everywhere in between, danced up a storm, hosted lots of parties, rollerbladed along the beach at sunset, aligned and balanced with yoga, gained clarity with journaling, opened up to dating and fell deeply in love. I also made more money that year than ever before.

When I became clear about the life I wanted I took the actions, both inner and outer, that helped me develop a strong sense of who I would be if I had the life I desired. Whether you want to co-create an entirely different life or bring about a single desire, the process is the same.

Even more good news—once you start living into your diamond essence, you'll help others find their own sparkle too. When my girlfriends witnessed my transformation, they were inspired to rediscover themselves, step outside of their comfort zone, and dive into their dazzle!

For example, at one of our many "get your magic mojo going" girl talk lunches, my friend Patti shared her desire to do something special and sexy for her husband's upcoming birthday. Being newly married she was clear about what she wanted—to have her man see her sensual side expressed in a new way giving him a pleasurable experience while creating a deeper level of connection between them. Maureen, Patti and I put our femme fatale minds together and had so much fun planning her amorous adventure. Since Patti loved to dance, performing a burlesque style show for him complete with props seemed a natural. With a theme in place we excitedly put together her costume, music and moves.

Patti was excited but nervous. To prepare she brought her sister over for moral support as she practiced. Between Maureen, Patti's sister, and myself, she had her support team in place. Plus she gave herself a lot of pep talks and saw the outcome she desired.

When the time came for her closeup, she almost chickened out. She had a fear her surprise might backfire. What if her husband laughed? What if it didn't play out the way she wanted? She didn't want to feel like a fool. Then she remembered her commitment to her friends along with her desired future and those things gave her a determined courage.

With blind faith Patti hit the "play" button of her recorder and as the music started she went for it. As she danced she relaxed and started feeling sensual and alive. When she was done she got the results she had envisioned. Her husband loved seeing this new sexy side, admired her bravery, and it took their closeness to a deeper level. The confidence she gained helped her step into the woman she had always wanted to be.

This first step of the SPARKLE System is ultra-important. It connects you with what you want and gives you the tools to co-create the life of your dreams. Use this process and the future *will* become the present. No dream is too big or out of reach. Simply see it, write it, talk about it, feel it, act on it, and live it! Keep your desires in the forefront of your mind at all times and don't let anyone take the wind out of your sails. Now filling in the details with the other SPARKLE steps will be easy and fun.

Pause and Reflect

1) Take some time to reflect on the question, "What would my life look like if I were living as an empowered sparkling sexy woman?" Give yourself permission to be bold and daring!
2) Do the exercise where you specify what the eight areas of your life would look like as your bright future. For audio guidance go to www.SexyandSparkling.com. When you are done journal as many details as possible about your experience. How do you feel about your future now? Ask yourself what outer and inner structures you will put in place to ensure attainment of this future.

3) What new languaging can you use when interacting with others to bring your ideal future to you sooner?

Revel in Your Radiance

Take what you've written about the ten areas of your life from exercise #2 above and put it on 3x5 cards. Keep them by your bed. Every morning when you wake up and every evening before you go to sleep, take about five minutes to focus on your desires. Close your eyes and visualize your desires already being fulfilled. These are the times your mind is most susceptible to taking in new thoughts. By doing it every day your subconscious has no choice but to make it happen for you.

If you find any limiting beliefs sneaking in to distract you like, "that will never happen for me," or "I'm too old," or "who am I kidding," don't fight it, just release it. Simply say, "in the name of Light, darkness be gone!" until the negative thought disappears and you are filled with peace.

Remember, when you envision yourself living the life you want to create—feel it in your core. The more intensely you feel it, the quicker it will show up in your life.

Chapter 5

P...Pinpoint Your Passions

Your heart is racing...your body exploding...joy, excitement and desire are bursting out of you like an uncorked bottle of bubbly. Baby, you've got lift-off! Pinpointing your passions and *living them* is the second principle of the SPARKLE system. This is a key element to your happiness.

Now, be honest. When's the last time you shouted "I'm ALIVE" to the world? If you've spent your life as a to-do-list diva or "people pleasing" addict, chances are, by the time you hit 40 you've buried your passions and forgotten what ignites your soul. I mean, really, how long has it been since you did what you loved, *without* feeling guilty?

Come on now, 'fess up—there is no right or wrong answer, this is solely for your awareness. But I will tell you this—if you're reading this book, you have a desire to get your sparkle on, and living a routine and robotic life will only dull you down. To get glitzy and glimmering you'll need to connect with your electric passionate energy.

In the last chapter you took the first step toward creating the life of your dreams. You visualized your magnificent future—all aspects of it. But were some parts vague or fuzzy? Are you still unsure of what you *really* want in some areas of life?

Passion involves discovering what excites you and opens you up—what feeds your soul. It also equates to feeling fully sensual, oozing your delicious goddess goodness. In this chapter you'll learn how to reconnect with both so you can manifest a life you love.

Falling in Love with Life

Once you overcome your fears you'll be free to live unedited. Can you imagine letting the real you bust through? It's going to be incredible because when you're bursting with passion everything you see is brighter, more vivid, and more colorful. It's as though you put on a magical pair of glasses and you're seeing things through a different lens. You've got this positive new perspective that's overflowing with a confident, "I can do *anything*" outlook.

And you'll find it doesn't matter if you're single or coupled up. Passion is about being *in love*...with life, a partner, a cause, an idea, an activity. There is no distinction between any of them; it's all the same energy. Have you ever noticed when one thing is going really well in your life everything seems to pop?

I'll give you an example. One of my students, Sylvia, signed up for my tele-playshop, "How to Find and Own Your Playful, Sexy Self." Her intention was to bring passion back to her marriage and life by breaking old patterns, getting out of her head and having more fun. At the time she was separated from her husband, working at a job she liked but didn't love, and felt disconnected from her feminine essence. Basically she wasn't enjoying her life too much.

During our work together she made some major shifts connecting with her feminine power and exploring her passions. She discovered her mission in life and began building a new career, and she renewed her spiritual foundation. Her entire outlook changed and she became super excited about her life. She went from a needy place to a faith-filled space. Magically, within a few months her husband wanted to reconcile. As she found passion in one area of her life, it spilled over into all the other areas.

By embracing those things that bring you bliss you'll suddenly notice your eyes are shining, your face is glowing, your heart is blossoming, and your essence is expanding. Fear fades, anxiety vanishes, and worries wash away. You are aligned with your truth. And when you are living in this larger-than-life space you are sending out waves of big beautiful positive energy magnetizing its match: love, happiness and joy.

Amazing opportunities and people will start showing up for you in the most marvelous ways. By designing a new paradigm of life for yourself, suddenly you'll have new powerful possibilities. Are you getting excited? Is there an awakening happening within your soul saying, "I want to live with passion now"? I hope so because you deserve nothing less. All you need to do is find it, feel it and live it!

Bliss List

You're probably wondering how to get to this coveted state.

Start by asking yourself, "What could I do for hours on end without getting paid that would fill me with joy and keep me spinning like a top?" Come from your heart and connect to that place and memory of what brings you bliss.

Write down five activities that make you really happy. Now assess each one—are they all dependent on other people or are the majority things you enjoy doing on your own?

If they are all dependent on other people you will have a challenging time to stay happy on a consistent basis as you are depending on others to get your "feel good." For example, if you say you are happiest when you are out on the town with your gal pals, what happens if your friends are suddenly unavailable? Do you find yourself a little depressed, sad, lonely?

On the flip side, if your five things are all based on activities you can do yourself—such as meditation/prayer, yoga, gardening, jewelry making, photography, etc.—then you are tapped in to the joys of your soul. Your mood and happiness come solely from you. And you are vibrating at optimal level. If stressful situations come up, you can easily handle them.

So, to stay sassy and spirited write out your five joys and make sure at least three of them are not dependent on others. Do at least one of them every day to maintain emotional and mental health. This is your happy pill!

After my divorce, I did a couple of things to help me discover my passions. I reflected on what I had always loved to do—travel, exercise, explore esoteric studies, and spend time with friends laughing and experiencing life. I tried new things that either related to my core passions or stretched me in some way. Yoga was a new way to exercise and the added benefits of spiritual alignment and balance and peace made it an instant new love. Then I began creating Romance-Capades—this was outside my comfort zone but proved to really ignite my soul's creative expression freeing me from my usual controlled state. Collaborating and creating with my friends also brought excitement, fun and fulfillment to my world. Studying alternative healing modalities such as Reiki, tuning forks and essential oils opened up a whole new world for me. Being curious and open to trying new things is crucial when looking to resurrect your passion.

What I learned is that the exploration of passion and its presence in my life helped to lift me out of stagnation, depression, confusion and the pain of my divorce. Doing those things I adored on a consistent basis took me out of victim mode and brought a new mindset that it was possible to have happiness and love again. It also gave me the knowing that I had the power of choice—live a life of passion or an endless pity party. Either way I designed my life. It was so much more uplifting and fun to choose to live with passion. You will find, as I did, living with passion empowers you to create a bright, beautiful and loving future.

Fun Adventures Journal

If you are not living with passion you are wasting the blessing of being alive. Starting a fun adventures journal not only helped me but many of my clients too. This is a place to note and write about anything and everything that gives you a feeling of renewed vibrancy. Choose a bold colored journal like red or yellow and make the outside as festive and exciting as possible. You want it to scream FUN so you'll be inspired to take action! Decorate using glitter pens, stickers, and any ornamentation that makes you feel happy.

On the front page make a list of those things you want to do but have never made the time for or had the courage to try— like belly dancing, pole dancing, a hot stone massage, a gourmet cooking class, photography, an outdoor festival or concert, a weekend getaway, eating chocolate naked, or traveling to an exotic destination. Every time you do something off your list put a heart sticker next to it or paint your lips with red lipstick and kiss the page. If you spontaneously did something wild and wonderful that's not on your list, give yourself double kisses. And then celebrate your action!

Make sure you journal about the feelings you had while engaging in the activity and definitely delve into what it awakened in you. You'll see simply getting outside of your normal routine will bring joy as well as confidence.

You'll want to make this tool a new habit, so commit to your fun adventures journal for at least 30 days and notice the difference it makes in the quality of your life.

Say yes to doing something fun every day—it could be something as simple as turning on your favorite song and dancing like a banshee for a few minutes, playing with your pet, singing in the shower, or having lunch with a friend. What do you like to do for fun? If you're drawing a blank, think back to when you were a kid—what made you giggle?

If that doesn't bring up any positive memories and you feel stuck start exploring. If you like chocolate try a dozen different types till you find the one you absolutely love. Visit a florist shop and see which flowers make you come alive. Pick up a local paper and look at the event section—what sounds interesting or fun? Google charitable causes; which one tugs at your heart and inspires the desire to volunteer? Pick up a community college catalog and see what classes sound interesting to you.

The point is, start trying different things and notice how your body feels when you are doing them. Do they bring you joy or leave you flat? This is how you will start connecting with your passions. Then commit to make living with vibrancy a daily habit!

If that sounds overwhelming you need to change your attitude because having joy in your life should be a priority like brushing your teeth. Actually you'll want to make it a top priority because when you do what you love you exude an energy that is irresistible. As you do more and more of what you love, you will create abundance in its highest form—a life that is fulfilling, alive, happy and full of love.

People are creatures of habit. When starting something new, like your fun journal, research shows daily participation makes you three times more likely to be successful than those who engage six days a week, and five times better than people who participate three, four, or five days a week.

If we become what we focus on, why not set your sights on fun, feminine, fabulous experiences?

Eidetic Imagery

Once you know what brings about enthusiasm and lust for life you can bring it into your future visioning. See yourself living with fire and fervor! Whether you are single and looking to meet that special someone or simply want to rev up your relationship, take the time to envision this for yourself and you will awaken your sensuality, creating a passionate life on purpose.

Using eidetic imagery coupled with a feeling of deep desire will help you embody your passionate Self. Eidetic imagery is when you visualize something with such clarity and perfection that it seems as though it's right in front of you. You vividly imagine the images, sounds, colors, objects and any other details that will burn it into your memory. Then add the feeling factor—how will you *feel* when this is all happening and you are at the center of this imagery?

Use the following four steps to create your eidetic image:

1) See yourself as the passionate being you want to be.
2) See the way you walk and talk.
3) See the way you connect with others.
4) See how others react and treat you.

How do you feel? Empowered, alive, vibrant? Visualize as often as possible throughout the day, acting as if this is already your life and soon that life will be yours. This is called owning it—you visualize what you want until it integrates and becomes your truth. From there, you live it!

Passion and Romance

Sensuality is another important dimension of passion—regardless of your relationship status. Sensuality is about the senses and is not to be confused with sexuality. Did you know we were born as sensual beings? Babies love to be held, fed, sung to and visually engaged. Unfortunately as we grow older we're often given beliefs that bring embarrassment about our sensuality, so we shut it down.

If you are disconnected from your sensuality, as many women are, a couple of things are happening. First of all you probably aren't getting a lot of male marveling. If you are shut down there is no opening, permitting them into your space. They feel this energetically without your saying a word and naturally keep their distance.

Secondly, you are probably looking for your man to bring passion into your relationship. Be honest, when he doesn't show up as Don Juan do you become angry, frustrated, resentful or disappointed because your romantic needs aren't being met?

The great news is you can remedy this by reconnecting with your sensuality and taking back your power. When you feel full in your Being and totally connected to the divine feminine, you experience a deep unearthing of raw, primal power. Think about when you've felt sensual—your senses were aroused and heightened, weren't they? Remember the physical sensations of inner warmth, opening and blossoming? Didn't your inhibitions go by the wayside while your womanly essence emanated out to mesmerize and captivate?

The truth is, the most attractive woman is the woman who loves life and values herself first. She feels desirable, full and ripe. Men see in her eyes that she "has it." She makes herself the priority and then the man. If she values the man more, she loses her appeal because she is not honoring and respecting herself first.

On a deeper level when you embody your sensuality, you develop personal intimacy. Since most women crave intimacy with a partner this is a crucial step, because it's impossible to share intimacy with someone else until you learn how to be intimate with yourself first.

Reawakening Sensuality

If you want to connect with your raw feminine essence take a few minutes and do the exercise outlined below. Tarnie Falloon, mind/body expert, first introduced me to this technique and since then I've added a few more layers that helped my clients make some very transformative shifts. I discovered engagement of more of the senses proved to be instrumental in opening the female heart center located within your pelvis and then connecting it to the main chakras brings a balanced sensual flow throughout the body. This was accomplished with the use of sound vibration (tuning forks) and essential oils—they really help to open and align. Guiding my clients through visualization was also hugely beneficial for juicification!

To open your sensual center start by getting very comfortable—either sit or lie down, whatever puts you in the most relaxed state. Set the intention that you are going to connect with your feminine essence. Close your eyes and take 10 deeply relaxing breaths all the way down to your hips.

Imagine you are breathing in a beautiful sparkling white light. As it travels down to your pelvis see this breath enlivening all your cells and caressing your female organs. As you exhale, release stale energy.

Begin to slowly and gently move your hips around as organically as possible while continuing to breathe into this area. You may want to start out in one direction and then shift to another. There is no right way to do this—simply intuit what feels best for you. Do this for two or three minutes, allowing yourself to open naturally.

What are you feeling? What are you sensing? Are you waking up delicious desires? Your body will talk to you so pay attention! After a few minutes you will feel the release of your innate sensuality moving through your body. This is the sensuality you are going for—nothing contrived or forced. We are looking to unleash your natural luscious Being.

Now open your eyes and notice how you feel. It may be subtle or it may be profound—whatever shift or change you are experiencing take a few minutes and write about it in your journal.

While at a retreat I used my version of this technique on Judy, mother of a nine-month-old baby. When she sat down with me, I saw a pretty woman but there was no passion in her eyes. At the end of this exercise, just 20 minutes later, when Judy opened her eyes she looked like she had just had a passionate romp with her lover. Her eyes were full of lustiness. She was smiling from ear to ear and told me it was very powerful for her—that she hadn't been connected to her sensuality since her baby was born. And now she was overflowing with a delicious vavoom.

The more you do this exercise the more you will connect with your personal power. Make it a part of your daily plan—just like brushing your teeth. This technique only takes a few minutes and the benefits are huge.

The best time to incorporate this practice into your day is right when you awake, before getting up. Most women have such long to-do lists they are running as soon as their feet hit the ground putting them in masculine action mode and taking them far, far away from their feminine foundation. So, before you get out of bed, still lying down, commit to spending a few minutes saying good morning to your magic mojo.

These days everyone has to get into action or nothing would get accomplished, but this way you start your day from a feminine vantage point. Since this is your natural state you might find you can accomplish your list with less stress and anxiety and actually get more done. You will feel balanced, peaceful and passionate allowing you to make decisions from your heart and intuitive state instead of your head in whatever you do.

One of my clients, Kathy, had been overworked for years, putting in 60-hour weeks. She wanted to quit to pursue her dream career but leaving a secure six-figure income without any savings kept her feeling nervous and stuck. However, after listening to the guided meditation consistently for a week she started trusting her gut instead of her head. She wrote her letter of resignation without any remorse and is now at total peace, doing what she loves.

This exercise is also excellent to practice if you are in a relationship and frustrated that the passion is gone. Feeling so naturally sexy you'll be sending out a vibe that will knock your man over and shift the dynamics.

For example, Mary, another client, had a tendency to feel more comfortable in her masculine energy. Although she experienced subtle sensations within her body she noticed big differences with her husband after doing this technique for only a week. He was talking more and telling her he just wanted to be near her. He was craving connection! For him to tell her this was totally different behavior. She was shifting her energy internally and her hubby was reacting to this new feminine essence. Give it a try and you'll see how it works like catnip and the sparks will start to fly again!

The great thing about this exercise is that it not only opens your feminine heart center it creates integration and flow of this sensual energy. If you prefer to be guided through this process go to www.SexyandSparkling.com.

Steps to Intimacy

Another great way to own your sensuality and become intimate with yourself is touch. When you let your hands slide over your body in a nonsexual way it brings a sacred, sensual encounter with your soul.

Close your eyes and touch your thighs, now your stomach and hips, arms, breasts. Thank your thighs for allowing you to walk every day, thank your hips for expanding to allow those beautiful babes into the world and/or give you that sultry saunter, and thank your stomach for reminding you that we live in a country rich with food...we are living with abundance. How lucky are you?

Once you have gained appreciation for your body with your eyes closed, stand in front of a mirror, eyes wide open and send love to every inch of your body. There is no judgment, criticism, loathing—just pure love. If you have a negative self-image this may be difficult at first but stay with it and repeat the exercise until you are comfortable and can look at yourself naked with unconditional love. When you are able to do this you will be able to embrace your life and love life with enthusiasm fully bringing YOU into the moment without any thoughts or insecurities that take away from your natural beauty.

Be grateful! When you start to appreciate your body you will start to feel more comfortable in your skin. With this comes peace—and with this comes a sizzling sensuality. So my beauty, start singing your praises, raise that vixen vibe, and soon you will be catnip for every man you meet!

Now is the time to cut loose and celebrate the honor and privilege of being a woman!

Ever see a woman walking with her shoulders slumped over, head down looking contracted? Don't you get the feeling she has low self-esteem? Or what about the woman who's walking so fast it looks like she's in a race? She's definitely engaged in her masculine energy. Now how about the woman who's walking slowly with purpose, head held high and shoulders back magnetizing every set of eyes for miles? There's something about that woman. The way she carries herself and the way she moves her body oozes sensuality. She's mesmerizing, isn't she? And what's most alluring about her is the way she owns her sensuality—with such ease and comfort.

Romantic Ruts and Their Roots

Has your relationship lost its passion? The truth is, due to disappointments and hurtful incidents with your mate you start to build walls around your heart for protection and you lose your connection—yes, from your partner but more importantly from yourself.

It's impossible to express or feel passion when you are focused on protecting yourself. You close off. You consciously blame someone else for your loss of luster not wanting to look at what's lurking beneath the surface in your subconscious.

Those core beliefs about yourself, unless healed, have a way of rearing their ugly heads, creating separation in your relationships. Whatever your recurring tape is—victim, martyr, narcissist, control freak—it keeps cropping up to create a tangled mess! Instead of facing it, most people choose to let it take them down the rabbit hole. This behavior is killing the passion in your relationship.

If you no longer have that WOW factor with your man and it's been ages since you've had "the tingles," take responsibility to create the passion you desire by tapping into your sensual Self. Once you start doing the things that bring you joy, your heart will open up again letting your beautiful essence flow out to the world, positively affecting your personal life and empowering you to build the bridge of connection you want in your relationship.

Touch like a Temptress

Once you've become intimate with yourself, you'll easily be able to develop intimacy with your partner. Even though most women long to hear the words "I love you," touch will help you create the closeness you crave in your relationships. Words are processed in the thinking part of your brain whereas touching goes directly to your emotional center.

Not only does touching create connection, it helps to calm the stresses of the day, adds a sense of caring and pleasure, and gets the endorphins flowing.

As part of your relationship romance plan set time aside every day to do at least one of the following:

1) Hug twice a day, a nice full body hug—none of this barely touching, Howard Hughes hugging. No, no, no. You've got to engage in a front on, full body hug—where you really hold each other, smell each other, and feel each other's heartbeat. The nurturing and caring involved in this embrace will slow you down enough to open the heart and relax into an intimate moment. Who knows where it might lead!

2) Kiss for at least 20 seconds. This will raise his testosterone levels and make you feel closer. A long, unexpected, sizzling smooch before he leaves for work in the morning will definitely get his juices flowing and you can bet he will not be working overtime tonight. Your sensual kiss will be lingering on his mind all day—he'll be counting the moments till he

can walk through the door and ravish you! Be ready!

3) Massage. The lips, hands, feet, and shoulders get emotionally stimulated when touched, so keep your relationship revved up with lots of lavish attention and tender touching.

If you put any of these tips into practice you'll be creating some stir—guaranteed! As you can see, you don't have to look like a super model to get a man's attention. Just let him catch the scent of your sensuality, confidence and playfulness and he'll be smitten.

When you are living with passion you will be in alignment with the Divine flow of life and in harmony with Spirit. Shine on, sparkling sister—any number of fabulous possibilities await you!

Pause and Reflect

1) Think back to when you were a child. What activities made you happy? Write about these in your fun journal.

2) Get your fun journal and list all the adventures you dream of having or experiencing. Jot down a start date and commit to doing something you enjoy every day.

3) What is limiting you from connecting with your sensuality? What steps can you take to overcome it?

Revel in Your Radiance

Feeling aglow with the fullness and wholeness of who you really are is your birthright! It's time to take that right back and live it daily. Listen to the feminine power guided meditation www.sexyandsparkling.com and then interact with a man. Did you notice any differences in yourself? What was his reaction to you? Spend a few minutes journaling your experience.

Chapter 6

A...Adjust Your Attitude

Have you seen the movie *The Holiday*, starring Kate Winslet and Cameron Diaz? It's one of my all-time favorites! Why? Because it gives a great message to women: live your life with the attitude that YOU are a leading lady.

Gumption, self-respect and the ability to consistently set clear boundaries that always honor your inherent value are the foundation of the leading lady persona. When you possess this attitude you never feel hopeless, helpless or victimized by the world. Instead you live as God intended you to—empowered to experience life in the highest and happiest way imaginable—kinda like *Star Power!*

So how are you living? Are you the leading lady of your life or are you the understudy, afraid to step into your greatness, complaining that you don't have what you want, blaming others for your lot in life; angry, sad, resentful, and bamboozled. It's all about attitude and the choices you make. You can shine from here to eternity if you adopt an attitude that embodies your magnificence! This is the third principle of the SPARKLE System.

Leading Lady Material

What I love about *The Holiday* is seeing the growth of Kate's character from heartbroken and depressed to confident and courageous. It's a great example of how changing your mindset and making positive choices has the ability to profoundly affect your attitude.

Let's look at the evolution of Kate's character. In the beginning of the movie she is devastated when her boyfriend unexpectedly announces his engagement to another woman at the office party. To heal her heartbreak she escapes to Los Angeles where she befriends a neighbor who is a wise, retired writer. Still raw, she confides in him, sharing the humiliation, devastation, deep pain and hurt she experienced when realizing this man she loved so dearly had been playing her all along.

Her new friend looks at her and says, "YOU are a leading lady, but you're not acting like a leading lady—you are acting like a supporting actress." Kate's character immediately gets it: she hadn't been living with the right attitude—an attitude that honored who she was and taught others to treat her with respect. She hadn't been embracing her magnificence.

Later in the movie, when her love interest tracks her down, Kate's character naively assumes he's left his fiancé. When she discovers he's still engaged, feigning confusion about his feelings, she finds her gumption, redefines her boundaries, and tells him what she thinks of him. Full of moxie she throws him out, slamming the door after him! She jumps into the air with glee and newfound freedom. She's found herself! Her victory is so palpable it could have been mine—I felt her triumph and cheered her with respect and admiration.

What does it mean to be a leading lady? If you think about the female "A" list stars in Hollywood they have an attitude that sparkles, don't they? They have gumption, are strong yet soft, and it's clear they love and respect themselves. There's a flowing energy that's wrapped around this core of strength that screams, "I am proud of me and honor who I am!" With confidence they navigate through the highs and lows of life and come out unbeaten. They put a stake in the ground when they get to the top of the mountain and stand ferociously for what they believe in. These ladies are unstoppable and so will you be when you adopt a leading lady attitude.

The Magic of a Good Attitude

When you have a good attitude people naturally want to be around you. When you are on a toxic binge watch everyone take cover and scatter! I know, life is full of obstacles and challenges—I can just hear you saying similar things as my clients, "But wait! What about when my husband trades cars with me and leaves me with no gas and a flat? Or how about when my daughter throws up on me just as I'm walking out the door for an important meeting? Or how about when my boss asks me to redo a report for the tenth time in a week?"

There are definitely countless things that can trigger us and cause emotional reactions, but when you let bad juju get the best of you, you're only harming yourself. Before you give into negativity, consider the consequences of how a bad attitude affects you:

1) It shortens your life. You actually take months if not years off your life when you consistently let negative emotions overtake you.
2) It creates an unpleasant future. If you constantly moan about and are dissatisfied with your circumstances, you're going to attract more of the same—*à la* the vicious cycle.
3) It harms others. Yes beauty, your negative mood affects the people around you. Whatever you're spewing and stewing over can be felt by others causing them distress and discomfort.
4) It produces negative effects. Every cause has an effect and your negative attitude causes negative circumstances. Many people think it's the other way around but honestly, it's your thinking that causes your circumstances.
5) It causes stress and robs you of peace of mind. And these can lead to anxiety, depression and health problems.

Ugh! There are lots of good reasons to flip that bad attitude into a good one. Yet a positive attitude is more than a delightful disposition. It's connecting to the fullness of who you are. It's a mindset that's steeped in making wise choices and feeling good about yourself when faced with challenges and negativity.

One weekend I had the pleasure of witnessing my client Amy adopt a fantastic attitude and use humor to overcome her fear. She was mesmerized by the leader of a seminar she was attending and wanted to find out if he was available, but her screaming meemies were rebelling big time. Determined to break her pattern she took a deep breath, gathered her courage, and sauntered over to her dream man. She smiled and asked if she could ask him a question. He was in a hurry and asked if it was a quick question. She assured him it was. Then she playfully told him a friend greatly admired him and loved his energy and wanted to know if he was available. Although he said he was in a "new" relationship his curiosity was piqued. Suddenly he had lots of time to find out more about this mystery woman! Who was she? When Amy playfully pointed to her own nametag, he was blown away and totally flattered. Afterwards Amy and I debriefed over drinks and she was positively giddy and glowing—she felt incredibly empowered.

That said, we are human and all fall prey to fear or a foul mood once in a while. Here are several tips and techniques to help you flip from a negative to a positive space:

1) Be of service and do something nice for someone else.
2) Listen to music that is uplifting—sound has the ability to shift your mood.
3) Use PSYCH-K—whole brain posture. Sit comfortably, cross ankles, cross wrists, palms facing each other, intertwining fingers. Close eyes and say, "I am happy," or "I am the purity that God desires" until you feel your body at peace.
4) Exercise.
5) Repeat the mantra, "In the name of Light, darkness be gone!"
6) Understand it's your evil twin trying to keep you from joy—outsmart her!
7) Invite your emotion to a tea party and have a heart-to-heart. Get to the bottom of your bad mood.

To teach yourself to stay in a positive mindset consistently, begin by asking yourself these three questions:

1) What message do I want to send about myself to my loved ones, friends, family, clients and new acquaintances?

How do I want them to feel when they are with me? (For example, that I'm loving, caring, wise, fun, joyful, intelligent, trustworthy, warm, strong, etc.)

2) How do I want my loved ones, friends, family, clients and new acquaintances to feel after they've interacted with me? (For example, respectful, inspired, admired, etc.)

3) What emotional energy do I want to add to the planet? Do I want anger, blame and resentment to flow from my heart or love, compassion and understanding?

Get as specific and detailed as you can because this will determine the energetic mix of your leading lady. It may be different for each group you interact with, but by getting specific on how you want to present and how you want people to feel, you become clear about your attitude. For example, if you want your husband to be more helpful around the house it's going to be far more advantageous to make him feel like your hero than nagging and complaining about his lack of effort. Perhaps you're interested in meeting a new guy. Rather than avoid his glance, a warm smile with eye contact will let him know it's safe to approach.

Minding Your Mindset

One morning while hiking I witnessed a physical example of how our mind works—it was fascinating. I noticed a woman walking her large and enthusiastic dog. She had him on a leash and was struggling to keep him in line. He was creating a whirlwind of challenging energy with his desire to check out every distraction. First he tried to chase a squirrel then he unexpectedly jumped into the air when he heard the birds singing, then he lunged at passing dogs on the street only to suddenly cross over to greet a gardener. His owner was struggling but successful in consistently reining him in.

My eyes were glued to this scene and even though it was exhausting to watch, the analogy was so clear. The dog was symbolic of our mind—so easily distracted without discernment. And like the woman, it is our job to put a short leash on our thoughts to keep them where we want them so we get where we want to go!

Our minds are fickle and fast. Is it any wonder we are so often drained when we don't control the distractions that take us from our positive mindset? How can we possibly sparkle when we are so disengaged?

To develop the attitude of a leading lady you must change and master your mindset. The most important thing about your attitude is your ability to manage it. Know that you have power over your thoughts and actions and you can choose positivity over negativity.

Use this four-step process to help you keep your mindset focused in a positive direction.

1) As you get up every morning make the conscious choice to face each day with inner strength and confidence in your abilities.

2) Set your intention to hold life-affirming thoughts all day because they will lead you to your highest good, saying things like:

   a. "I choose to embrace this God-given day with a positive attitude."
   b. "I choose to look at life with enthusiasm and fresh eyes.
   c. "My attitude has a wonderful and powerful influence

on my day."

d. "My attitude affects the relationships and the outcomes I experience in the most blessed way."

5) Create a vision for the day. See yourself responding to life with a new and positive attitude and in return receiving abundant blessings.

6) Maintain awareness throughout the day. When you notice your mind wandering into the dark, rein it back into the light.

Light always trumps darkness—so if you feel yourself slipping, go back to this four-step process and ask the Divine/Source or whatever you believe in to help you bring forth your emotional and mental strength.

Find a Role Model

When I re-entered the dating world I realized I had to make some changes that were uncomfortable for me—like flirting and dressing in a more fetching style. I had to get a new mindset going to pull this off. Just like the dog, one minute I was running in the direction of "I can do this! " and the next my stomach was in knots and I was telling myself "No you can't."

My discomfort and inability to remain consistently open to a new way of being became my biggest obstacle. Despite my knowing I needed to adopt a healthier attitude about developing this sensual side of myself I grappled. However, instead of beating myself up for not knowing how to change, I made a wise decision and reached out for help to a couple of friends who were naturally "those kind of women." You know, the ones who have it all going on, the women other women watch and go "WOW!"

These women's secrets were daunting for me to take action on. With each uncomfortable step I was scared, nervous and wanted to throw up, but I mustered the courage and did it. Although I wouldn't say I ever became "one of them" I gradually gained confidence and became comfortable allowing this side to surface. And what I loved was discovering a different attitude can be learned if you apply yourself and make the effort.

I'm not suggesting you are not enough on your own or that being someone else is better; however, if you are currently an understudy wanting to become a leading lady but have no idea how to do that, you are going to need some mentoring. The exciting news is it's possible! All you have to do is make different choices and take actionable steps to get you there. If you have a friend like I did enlist her help. If not find a role model, someone you admire and say, "I know that personality is in me—I've been a little shy and scared to bring it out, but now I'm ready." Dig in and find her! Study the behavior of your favorite star. Then test it out, and when you are comfortable add your own personality so that it becomes your unique attitude.

Please don't fall into the trap of comparing yourself—it will just make you feel less than. Instead take note of the traits you admire and say, "I can do that!" Being inspired by others is God's gift to you—His way of giving you an example to learn from so that you will know how to manifest the same in your life.

Whether you are in awe of a celebrity, public figure, relative, or friend frame a picture of them and place it in clear view so that you are reminded of the traits you want to bring forth and embody. Write down the aspects of their attitude that you are enamored with. In order to adopt the same character you will need to know what it is that you admire so much. Take time every day to look at the photo of this idolized figure and say out loud, "I honor your traits of ______________ , and know I can own them too!" Then spend a few minutes and feel what it would be like to possess those qualities.

This action sends a powerful message to your subconscious instilling the new demeanor you desire.

Stepping into Your Leading Lady

Give yourself permission to explore and expand. The truth is you are layered with depth from the many experiences you've had and through it all you've developed many different personality flavors. Some you engage on a regular basis, but the others stay buried. Start your discovery and let them all come out to play!

All these beautiful facets of your personality are the leading ladies that live within you—waiting to get a taste of life and shine. But you habitually let the same ones star in your movie and tell the same story. It's time to write a new script, so be bold and daring and give the personas you've been hiding a chance to glitter and sparkle.

Allow yourself to be creative, to play, to have pleasure, to enjoy, to love your life. Say yes to stepping into the leading lady you want to become...give yourself the freedom to be totally uninhibited and when you do that you will start to feel young and ALIVE again!

One of my clients, Janine, did a brilliant job of this. She and her husband of 30-plus years were having a lot of marital problems. They had been living like roommates for several months and nowhere near as close as she desired. She had just enrolled in a course with me and decided to listen to one of the bonus calls with a sensuality expert who gave lots of tips on how to seduce your man without saying a word.

One night she decided to try out a suggested seductive pose, called "the stand," along with other flirty techniques she learned. When she heard her husband drive up she got into a curvy, sexy pose but he barely noticed her. She didn't take it personally because she remembered the expert saying men need a woman to look at them at least four times before they "get it." God love her, she did not give up! Instead she patiently continued to pose every chance she got and, even though her husband wasn't responding in the way she wanted, she started feeling really good about herself. Suddenly, after 90 minutes, he locked eyes with her; they flirted and kissed and had the most passionate night she could remember in ages! She was giddy with excitement and shared that she felt sensuous, feminine and fabulous.

Janine most definitely gets the Leading Lady Award. She did not allow her husband's initial non-responsiveness to shut her down. Instead she started to feel good about herself and continued for her own enjoyment. It's no coincidence that he noticed and wanted her exactly when she got to this point—she was dwelling in the sweet spot of her magnificence without any external need of attention.

That's the secret we learn: When we're in right relationship with ourselves, all good things flow to—and from—us. The next chapter will show you how to renew your connection with your feminine, fabulous Self.

Pause and Reflect

1) Write down what it would take for you to step out of understudy and step into being the leading lady of your life? What stops you? What structures do you need to put in place to live as a leading lady?

2) What is your big payoff in being the understudy? What do you get out of it? You have to get something out of it or you wouldn't be doing it.

3) List 10 traits that you want people to name when describing you.

4) Now that you know how important it is to master your mind, what three tools can you use to keep yourself on a short leash? How will you turn negative thoughts into positive?

5) Choose your leading lady role model, study her behavior and list the traits you want to embody.

Revel in Your Radiance

For inspiration check out movies where the leading lady starts off without acceptance—be it social, physical, economic, intellectual or romantic—and by the end not only finds but completely redefines herself – you may just find you will be motivated to do the same!

1) *Baghdad Café*: No glamour gal or beauty queen, Brenda is just an average woman—meaning she is like you or me. The genius of the character's evolution is that she becomes

a fascinating, sexy woman just by taking action steps that create confidence within her.

2) *How Stella Got Her Groove Back*: A steamy romance during an island vacation prompts Stella to reevaluate—and reinvent—her life.

3) *Erin Brokovich*: In the beginning she's a blue-collar girl who can't get a job. By the end she's engaged all her abilities to bring a billion-dollar corporation to its knees.

4) *Working Girl*: Tess is seen as corporate eye candy but by using her persistence and intelligence she refuses to be chewed up and spit out.

5) *Last Holiday*: When she is erroneously given a fatal diagnosis, Georgia sets out to live life with gusto—doing all the things in her "someday" binder. She quits her job, travels to Europe and lives totally outside the box—taking all the risks she had dreamed of doing but never had the courage to act on before.

6) *The Holiday:* When love goes bad two women living on two separate continents exchange homes to heal their hearts and discover what it takes to become the leading lady of their lives – finding their gumption they redefine the boundaries they've been living by and find the love they desire - never to settle for crumbs again.

Chapter 7

R...Renew Your Relationship with YOU!

When you think about it, life is about relationships. Every minute of every day you are relating with someone or something—be it your partner, kids, boss, co-workers, friends, family, store clerk, stranger, pet, computer, car, Self—the list is endless.

And the most important relationship of all? You guessed it—your relationship with yourself. If you've lost your sparkle, somewhere along the way you've abandoned yourself and will need to renew your relationship with *you*. Without a solid partnering with yourself, you'll never be able to successfully connect with others. So you want to be sure your personal foundation is built on love, trust, honor and respect. This is *bar none* the most important and pivotal connection for you to develop. Your happiness depends upon it!

If you are like most women over 40 you've put yourself on

the back burner so many times you begin to feel guilty doing anything "me" oriented. The abandonment of yourself came naturally—you made everyone else a priority. How many times have you felt like you're going to pop, but instead of doing something nurturing for yourself you ignore your needs to cater to your kids or a friend? And then there's your partner's needs—are you the type that puts his needs and requests before your own? Maybe you've given up your free time to take care of your aging parents, or perhaps you've never set boundaries with your boss and are being worked like a dog. Sound familiar? This is how you lost yourself. This is how your dazzle dimmed.

In this chapter we talk about the importance of how you relate to *you*. The key to your sparkling happiness begins with building a rock solid relationship with YOU! It's crucial, honey child! This chapter will show you how.

How Do You Treat Yourself?

Are you your biggest and brightest fan or your own worst enemy? Do you applaud your accomplishments or do you look at what you didn't get done? When you're tired do you stop to nurture yourself or do you push yourself harder with nothing ever being good enough? In other words, do you accept, respect, and love yourself? If you don't honor yourself, how can you expect others to love and respect you? You teach others how to treat you by how you treat yourself. So there's no time like the present to start your deep diving discovery.

Ask yourself, "Do I value myself as much as I value my children or best friend?" If the answer is no, you'll want to look at behavioral patterns that started in childhood. I know, I know, everyone tells you to go back to childhood, but there's a good reason for it. You learn to talk to yourself the way your parents talked to you as a child. If you grew up in a home where your family was always judging and blaming you for something or you suffered from verbal abuse, or you only felt loved when you accomplished something, you can bet you've carried that baggage into your adulthood.

Famed scientist Bruce Lipton talks about how it's been proven your mind is in a hypnotic state until you are about six years old, taking everything in as truth. As a child you don't have the ability to discern fact from fiction so if you believe everything your parents and authority figures tell you—holy moly, how are you ever going to sparkle? If your parents doled out detrimental beliefs, slowly but surely the truth of who you are got buried and you developed an unhealthy relationship to yourself.

But here's the great news: their beliefs were based on their own experiences and had nothing to do with you! And they meant no harm—they were just seeing things through their own lens and have no other perspective to draw upon. Nevertheless, the negative tapes you have running in your mind are junk. The faster you realize this and release them, the quicker you'll be living your luscious life.

What you must get is that all the bad beliefs you grew up accepting about yourself are not who you are. The reality is you were born perfect with a brilliant diamond of light at your core. This is your unique essence, your truth. You don't have to do anything to prove your worth. Just being you, right here, right now, means you are incredibly special and valuable.

This acknowledgement and understanding will fill you with love, compassion, wisdom, and gratitude. When you understand these are your authentic foundational qualities you are free of the limiting tapes. This is your truth. As you practice and become these principles, you not only build a beautiful relationship with yourself, almost simultaneously you develop the warm and intimate relationships you desire with everyone and everything in your life.

Making It to the Mountaintop

I recently had an experience that strengthened my relationship with me. I was in Beaver Creek, Colorado for a fun girls' trip and on the second day we planned a special lunch at the celebrated restaurant, Zach's Cabin. Because I've had two hip replacements I chose not to join my girlfriends in skiing. While they would simply ski down to the eatery it was suggested I snowshoe up.

My friend Vicki, a seasoned marathon runner, told me it would take a mere 20 to 30 minutes—an easy trek! Barely out of a bout with bronchitis and nowhere near as in shape as Vicki, I had my doubts. Feeling a little nervous about the whole venture I toyed with chickening out and taking the gondola. But I didn't want to look like a wimp (yes, I still have to work on my limiting beliefs), so I geared up for the challenge. Shifting my attitude was the first thing I did to get out of self-doubt. Since I love to exercise I chose to look at it as a fun adventure.

I gave myself triple the time Vicki estimated to lose the stress of being late. Feeling full of moxie with gear in hand, I made my way to the nearby resort to get a map of the mountain. Clear about my destination I strapped on my snowshoes with excitement. But as I stood at the base of the mountain I was overwhelmed by its steepness and fear started talking. "Are you crazy? You can't do this. Just take the gondola."

It was a fight, but soon I was able to quiet the sludge sisters down, set my mind to success and begin my trek. But before long they were back, singing, "Ay yi yi, what did you get yourself into?" Within minutes I was gasping for air—oh yeah, never factored in the altitude! My heart was pounding so hard I thought it would bust out of my chest but I persisted. I started playing mental games with myself—if I take 70 steps I can stop and catch my breath and look at my progress. I was only halfway there and I could feel my legs turn to jelly—I knew I couldn't quit but I seriously didn't know how I was going to make it.

I started to use every mental trick I could think of. I had read saying the word "yes" energizes and gives you power so I tried that and it worked, but only for another 210 steps. Man, oh man, how was I going to make it up this mountain? I needed the big guns so I started a mantra of gratitude to God—with every step I said, "Thank you for giving me strength, endurance and stamina." Instantly I felt my body strengthen and I was now able to go 100 steps before I needed to catch my breath. Empowered with Divine energy, I made it to Zach's with five minutes to spare.

I was so proud of myself for overcoming my naysayer mind, persevering to the top and remembering to use my mental tools I took off my snowshoes, jumped in the air and let out a big wooohooo! It was a tremendous accomplishment for me and I felt something shift inside—a new layer of confidence emerging and validating success is a mindset. I was reminded that if I put my mind to something, success will follow—including this book that I've been talking about writing for 12 years. What a lesson!

What I learned and want to share is that taking on something challenging, asking for the help you need, and seeing it through to completion will seriously strengthen your relationship with you, helping you believe and trust in your abilities and know you are not alone. It's as powerful as the brilliant diamond you are!

Improving Your Relationship with Yourself

We are always relating whether we think we are or not. Even if you don't verbalize anything your thoughts are energy and affect your body and the airwaves. So you want to make sure you keep your thoughts pristine! When you have a snarky thought it doesn't just stay in an airtight container within your mind—oh no. It leaks out and not only pollutes your body creating disease but pollutes the world too. Think about the 8.9 earthquake in Japan in 2011—the energy of this shaker carried to the California coastline creating fear of potential tsunamis. The same is true of your thoughts and emotional energies—they do some traveling and affect others.

Since you were born to be red carpet radiant, you'll want to clear that clutter so you can grace the airwaves with your brightest star essence. That means you'll need to treat yourself as the precious being you are—with kindness, compassion and patience. And you'll need to accept, love and approve of yourself completely. I know you can do this!

Body Beautiful

Let's start with your body. In order to build a great relationship with yourself, you must love your body fully, wholly and unconditionally. If you don't, that's a message that there is some healing needed in order to shift that "not so nice" perspective you have goin' on. Because you know what? That attitude is not doing you a lick of good in living your best life, in achieving your goals and in how you are presenting to others. If you think there is something off about you, others are going to pick right up on that vibe and mirror your thoughts right back to you.

I understand this battle and the emotions involved—it brings back memories of everything I went through to release 40 pounds several years ago. I know body image is a biggie! I knew this topic had to be in the book because in order to live, laugh and love with freedom, you need to feel really good about your body image. And I don't just mean your physical size. I'm talking about every lovely inch of your body, head to toe, sista! That means hair, nose, eyes, hands, feet, hips and thighs, derriere, cellulite, and those scattered, funky freckles!

So, what kind of relationship have you got going on with your body? Do you adore and respect your every luscious curve? Are you appreciative of all it does for you? Do you pay attention to what it needs—eating nutritiously and exercising so you're at your optimal health?

Here are a few tips to help you love your beautiful body—even before you start working to release a few pounds, tone, or reshape it:

1) Look in the mirror and really get that you are a creation of perfection. You are beauty incarnated and nothing else. Give yourself a little wink and a smile and say, "Hello, gorgeous!"
2) Make a list of at least five things you like about your body and carry that list with you. Have it on hand so you can quickly pull it out whenever you need to remind yourself

how incredible you are. Remember, focus only on your fabulousness!

3) See yourself at your desired weight. Notice the way you walk and talk. What are you wearing? See the way you connect with others and envision how others treat you. Hold court, girl! Hold that vision as often as possible throughout the day. Soon that fantasy will be your reality.

Maybe you already love yourself and are unleashed. If so, celebrate! But if you struggle in this area I encourage you to practice the above three empowering suggestions. Also, come from a place of appreciation of where you are today—that will help you move forward faster.

That said, there's no getting around it: after 40 the body starts to do a slip-slide, doesn't it? Ay yi yi and how! I remember thinking it would never happen to me—boy, was I arrogant and wrong. After going through an early menopause, things shifted, dropped, pouched, and spread seemingly overnight—it was either laugh or cry!

Whether you are battling with a loss of hormones or not, the body starts to rearrange itself. So this is a time in your life when it's important to accept and love yourself, honoring your body as the *goddess temple it is,* regardless. Embrace a new theme in regards to body image and look at exercise as a way to stay fit and strong for internal health. Staying physically active also helps in keeping your confidence high and your spirits up—it worked for me big time after my divorce.

When my marriage broke up I told my trainer I wanted to get into awesome shape. At first it was ego, wanting to look as good as I could so that when I saw my ex he would be sorry he left me—okay, I admit, totally childish revenge. Fortunately I soon had a different motivation. Exercise helped me feel strong, replaced my self-pitying thoughts with positive inspirational visions, and plied me with confidence and courage. Ah, to feel good about myself again! When I added yoga to the mix I felt even better—it was like coming home.

The first time I practiced yoga I left with such a high I felt like I was floating for three days. Reaching mind/body and soul alignment cleared my mind of chaotic thinking and brought a blissful peace that was priceless. It also introduced me to my body in a way weight training and other physical sports had never done. The movements were sensual and intimate, and I became aware of how my breath travels to awaken and open every nook and cranny. I felt energy being released and moving through me as well as the flowing of my blood. Yoga helped me connect with my inner world. How do you connect with yours?

Make sure to choose exercises that you enjoy so you'll be more likely to include them in your life. If you want to be out there hiking and biking into your later years, you'll want to adopt a passionate and spirited attitude about health and fitness:

- Choose exercises that you enjoy and view as FUN.
- Try new hikes to keep it interesting and exciting.
- Schedule exercise so you get it into your day without excuses.
- Make healthy food choices—saying sayonara to white flour products and sugar.
- Visit a wellness store and get a good supplement plan going that's doable in all ways.

This is your new 24-Carat Body Beautiful strategy—the key being, *it has to be fun and it has to be realistic.*

Forgiveness

Just as important as renewing your relationship with your body, it's crucial to get rid of all the emotional and mental baggage that's been weighing you down, keeping you small and dimming your light. Similar to a nice sugar scrub washing away the dead skin and polishing it to a new glow, forgiveness is a way to give yourself a fresh start.

The truth is every woman at her core is as valuable as a diamond, but few realize it because they are too busy racing through the day trying to fit everything in: career, laundry, grocery shopping, soccer practice, helping with homework, straightening the house, volunteering, cooking dinner, supporting a friend or family member. Basically, taking care of everyone else. With all this doing vs. being, a woman can begin to look and feel more like a diamond in the rough than someone who has a special spark about her.

At this point in your life you probably realize all the focused energy on accomplishment has not brought the happiness you thought it would. As a matter of fact, you might have built up some angst and may even feel trapped in a prison of anger, resentment, blame and pain.

And then there's the guilt for feeling any of those emotions! I know. I've been there. As soon as you decide to stand up for yourself and set some boundaries, a taunting voice goes off in your head—*You're selfish! You're a horrible person! Who do you think you are?* To fight back you may throw yourself a little pity party, go into justification, or select martyrdom, none of which are healthy.

Through my own personal experience and the women I coach it's been pretty amazing to see all the buried anger. Their total denial of this rage is understandable because, after all, good girls don't get angry, right? Wrong. Again, I know. I've been there. How do you think I can see it so clearly?

Wouldn't it be nice to be free of all those burdensome emotions that weigh you down, possess your mind, close your heart, and stress your body? You can, through forgiveness.

Forgiveness is a gift you give to yourself. It isn't something you do for someone else. As Lewis Smedes put it, "To forgive is to set a prisoner free and discover that prisoner was you." Yet many people feel that if they forgive someone for hurtful things that were said or wrongdoings, the other person wins—it's as if you're letting that person off the hook.

I get it—during and after my divorce I had a lot of anger I didn't want to get rid of. When well-meaning friends told me to forgive, I thought they were excusing my husband and his new lover who had caused me all the pain. My first reaction was, how could I forgive two people who consciously destroyed my life? Oh no, that was not going to happen because I was very attached to my victim role!

But something deep inside of me told me to explore this concept. It resonated at a soul level despite my ego's resistance. As I read different books I discovered the most important person I needed to forgive was myself. This was a revelation—the fact that I might need to forgive myself had never crossed my mind. I was so committed to blaming my ex I didn't have to expose my part in the demise of our marriage. Blaming him also helped me hide that I was terrified there was something wrong with me, I wasn't enough, I might be the horrible person he said I was and that's why he left me. It was years before I was able to forgive myself for buying into that belief. I wasted a lot of time, and I don't want you to fall into that same trap.

As Buddha said, "Holding onto anger is like grasping a hot coal with the intent of throwing it at someone else. You are the one who gets burned." You may remember what happened for the rest of your days, but when you forgive you lessen the grip of negative emotion the incident has on you. This will help you to focus on positive aspects of your life so you CAN move forward.

On the flip side if you've done something that needs to be forgiven and you are holding onto it with a vice grip, what does this do to you? Fills you with tremendous guilt, right? *How could I have done that? How could I have said that? I'll never forgive myself for...* This just leads to the blame and shame game, which is another trick of the mind to hold you back and prevent you from moving forward with happiness. Not to mention the hit your self-esteem and self-worth take. Allow yourself to forgive YOU!

So many women wrestle with guilt. If you are one of them ask yourself this question, "Who would I be without the guilt?" Get to the root of what holds you to the guilt because without it you are a new woman—light, sparkling and free.

The grudges you hold onto for all the injustices done to you have kept you angry but the person you are most angry at is yourself—for getting into *that* situation again—for not paying attention to those big ol' red flags, for not standing up for yourself, for saying yes when you really wanted to say no, for sacrificing so much, for being too cautious and not jumping on opportunities, for listening to other people, for being a doormat, for being a pleaser, and so on.

What I've learned is that all forgiveness is self-forgiveness but sometimes we need to start with forgiving others to get the process going. Ask yourself these questions if you find yourself resisting letting go:

1) What is my payoff for holding on to these thoughts?
2) Who would I be without the "I've been wronged" song I've been singing?
3) By hanging on to the negative emotion, what part of my life am I not taking responsibility for?

When you're unable to find forgiveness your heart is in a closed state, and it's impossible to be your beautiful Self when there is such heaviness weighing you down. That negative vibration of your thoughts is attracting more negative stuff and creating a vicious cycle that only spirals downward. Only love and the forgiveness you find as a result of opening your heart will lift the pain of the past.

When you forgive you are at your sparkling best and it's your pathway to love. As Mother Teresa said, "If we really want to love, we must learn how to forgive."

Take a moment and think about a situation that needs to be forgiven. Ask yourself, "Am I willing to waste my energy further on this matter?" If the answer is NO, the process of forgiveness can begin.

Developing Self-Love

Honor all that you are! Here are some tips for developing self-love:

1) Write yourself a love letter. I mean really gush all over you. You are digging for your diamonds here so get out your pick, put on your mining hard hat and start excavating. If this is hard for you or you draw a blank ask a good friend or family member to help you discover your dazzle.

2) Combat the critics. Ah yes, the stealth committee of your mind—always at your service to run you over the coals. When they show up *en force* simply say, "Thank you for sharing, but no thanks! I choose to live with brilliance not bullying."
3) Speak your truth—at all times, no matter what. Even if you think the conversation will be hard, show up with honesty and come from love. This honors who you are as well as the recipient.
4) Practice self-care. Listen to your body and take care of your needs! Eat when you're hungry, sleep when you're tired, get a massage, indulge in a mani pedi, exercise, and kick any destructive habits/addictions like alcohol, drugs, and food abuse. You may need a village to help you and that's okay. Don't be afraid to reach out—you are worth it! There is plenty of support waiting to help you shine.
5) Accept yourself—no matter what your race, color, height, or gender, just accept the facts. You cannot change these things. If you don't accept them you will cripple yourself—let go of what you cannot change and choose to celebrate instead.
6) Find evidence that supports how wonderful you are!

Every day you are going to be faced with situations that challenge your state of being, but when you understand that your heart inherently holds the blueprint for love, joy and happiness and all you have to do is tune in, you'll discover you're not so burdened when things go awry. And ultimately, when you fall in love with YOU, your world will too!

Once you've forgiven yourself and fallen in love with you, you're ready to develop those delicious connections with others. But first take a look at how you relate to others. If you are single and want to be married but you are independent and living an isolated life, how are you going to bridge that gap?

If you want intimacy you'll need to learn to share your feelings as they arise instead of scurrying off to recharge your battery and work things through on your own. To become what you dream yourself to be, you'll need to step outside your comfort zone and take actions that are in alignment with the person you want to become. Hang out with married couples, share your feelings, make time in your life for a mate, make physical space for a partner, meet new people, carpool. As you take the steps that move you towards your vision you will bridge the gap.

One of my clients, Heidi, took a huge step to move toward her desire for more romance with her boyfriend. She came to one of our very first romance parties. At first, she was a mousy little woman who seemed to be afraid of her own shadow. She wanted romance but didn't know what to do. She also wanted her relationship to go to the next level.

So one night when her boyfriend was working late, she had a picnic basket sent to him filled with three items...his favorite dessert placed on a pretty pair of panties and a key to her apartment deliciously dangling. The next day we set up her apartment with rose petals, tons of candles, and romantic tunes. She was very nervous but wanted things to change so badly she was able to overcome her fears and stay focused on creating a magical night. She made all the things he loved to eat and when he arrived he was completely surprised and touched that she had done all of this for him. By bravely stepping out of her comfort zone, Heidi not only added romance to her relationship, but also gained confidence and began to see herself in a whole new light.

Building relationship with yourself by releasing what no

longer serves you and practicing forgiveness will help you develop self-love. This will give you an irresistible inner sparkle magnetizing all the joy and happiness you can imagine.

Spiritual Connection

Conflict, mistrust, and busyness all lead to isolation, disconnection, and loneliness. The pain that shows up in your life from these actions and behaviors is the great pain of separation from God/Source/The Divine, or whatever you believe in, and Self.

If you're not connected to yourself it's impossible to connect with anyone else. You can try but it will always land flat. Tapping into you is the way you flip your switch. Not only will your result be juicy, it's the key to soul-to-soul connection.

When you are spiritually connected you will save yourself a lot of time and energy and misery by recognizing what feels right to say yes to. You are always being guided with gentle nudges. Pay attention and life will be so much easier! For example, you won't let your loneliness win out when you meet the guy who looks good on paper but to whom you feel no connection. You won't take that job that pays well but makes your stomach churn. When you are in tune with your inner sparkle, your relationships and life path will be much easier and a lot more fun.

Developing a deeply loving relationship with yourself will enable you to create the same incredible partnerships with other people. If, however, you don't have a great relationship with yourself, you'll be out there feeling frustrated and disrespected, convinced there's something wrong with you.

Fortunately, returning to love is easy when you realize that love is and always has been within you all the time. This is your Diamond Power—your divinity—that sparkling essence that is uniquely you. Remember how the Tin Man in *The Wizard of Oz* was in search of his heart, certain the great and powerful Oz was the only one who could give it to him? Then he discovered it was there within him all the time!

The same is true for you. The loving life that you want starts when you start loving YOU. *Be* love and you will *have* love. It all starts with you—knowing you are lovable, knowing you belong, knowing you are part of the all, knowing you are enough, needed and wanted. Love will lift you out of pain and soften the harshest moments. Just like Dorothy, you've got to click those sparkling ruby stilettos, believe in your loving essence, and you will find your way home.

Pause and Reflect

1) Sit in a quiet place, close your eyes and give yourself a huge hug by wrapping your arms around yourself. Love on yourself until you feel warm and juicy inside.

2) Play the bracelet game. Make or buy three to five elasticized bracelets and put them on one wrist. Every time you say or think a judgment, criticism or negative thought, move a bracelet to the other wrist. The goal is to go 21 days without moving a bracelet.

3) Make a sugar scrub out of honey and raw sugar and brush away all the dead skin. As you do so imagine you are scrubbing off all the negative clinging issues that make you

feel unlovable. Repeat as often as desired—you'll feel fresh, polished and pretty.

4) What do you need to forgive? Make a list and let the healing begin by putting your hand over your heart and saying, "I forgive myself for buying into the belief that I'm ________." "I forgive myself for judging ____________ for ________________."

5) The next time you feel disconnected and lonely, reach out and communicate with someone.

Revel in Your Radiance

To start an intimate relationship with yourself, sit quietly, imagine a beam of pure, sparkling Divine white light coming down from the heavens and entering your body. As this light touches the core of your Being, see your soul light up just like a Tiffany diamond showcased under the brightest of lights—its brilliance taking your breath away. When you connect to this energy, fully feeling it and befriending it, you will understand who you *really* are and start to build a relationship of honor with yourself. Get to know YOU and your MAGNIFICENCE, and you will become your biggest fan.

Chapter 8

K...Know Who You Are

Have you ever lost yourself? I mean really reached the point where you didn't remember who you were anymore? After my marriage ended that realization was one of the most painful moments of my life. Working so hard for material gain I built my persona on a false foundation and created a woman I no longer recognized. Instead of standing strong in the center of my authentic value, I defined who I was by my career success and other people's opinions. Just like a chameleon I changed to become who and what I thought others wanted me to be, always seeking outside approval.

In losing sight of me, I disconnected from my divine value, my diamond power. I don't want any woman to lose herself like I did for as long as I did. My passion in writing this book is to provide you with a system that will support you when faced with curve balls and help you remember who you are at all times—a magnificent, beautiful, brilliant woman as valuable as a diamond.

If you're wondering, as I once did, what it means to live with the knowledge of who you are, let me define it for you:

1) You allow yourself to shine as brightly as the sun.
2) You're fully Self-expressed and choose to live out loud, totally engaged with life.
3) Your masculine and feminine energies are balanced.
4) You feel alive and vibrant knowing that your radiance defies age and physical imperfections.
5) You live with confidence and courage not caring what anyone thinks.
6) You are comfortable in your own skin—never trying to be someone else.
7) You're so sure of your value that other people's opinions and comments don't cause you to waver.
8) You do not give up on yourself no matter what obstacle you encounter.
9) You remember and honor why you're here.
10) You share your talents and gifts with the world.
11) You connect and give to others.

When you are solidly living in this state, the need for outside approval will fly out the window because you are aligned with the deepest truth of who you are. Wooohooo! Without a doubt, the "K" is the most crucial cornerstone of the SPARKLE System.

The Trap of External Validation

Think about this for a minute…how do you get your value? Do

you know who you are without all the identities you've taken on since birth? Are you able to accept and honor you just for being you without the labels of daughter, sister, mother, wife, friend, student, grandmother, entrepreneur, etc. Do you have an identity that's not dependent on your accomplishments or external validation? Can you feel worthy without feeling like you have to earn it?

When I got hip to how my external needs played out behaviorally I started noticing a whole lot of women doing the same thing. The biggest consequence is that it's very disempowering and doesn't allow us to freely give of our gifts and talents to the world.

When you aren't able to love, accept and appreciate yourself, you're like a junkie looking for someone to give you your next fix. When you get it, you feel good about yourself but it's like any high—short lived. The second it's gone and you find yourself doubting your significance, the hunt is on again until you get your next fix and the next and the next. It's an exhausting never-ending needy cycle that leaves you disrespecting yourself time and time again.

Letting someone else determine your value is a way you give your power away and set yourself up for misery. When you carry the core belief, "I'm not enough" or "I'm not worthy" or "I'm not lovable," nearly every interaction you have will confirm your fear. Your outer world is always a direct reflection of your inner world.

You may have heard everything is energy, including your beliefs—and they carry a certain energetic vibration that magnetizes the people, events and situations to you that match the vibration of your belief. Until you break these negative energetic patterns you will keep attracting the same unwanted situations day after day after day!

Have you ever entered into a relationship without knowing who you are, expecting your partner to make you happy and give you your value? If you answered yes you probably experienced feelings of anger, insecurity or resentment when your partner didn't feed your needs and maybe even began to believe *he* was to blame for the relationship not working when in reality you had not entered feeling whole, solid in Self-love.

If you frequently say things like, "Where are you going?" "Why are you late?" "Don't leave me," and complain you get your feelings hurt a lot, there are probably painful past experiences yet to be healed. This is also a sign you are not connected to your innate diamond power. Consequently the relationship starts to feel heavy instead of happy.

When you go into a relationship looking to "get" rather than "give" without any self-appreciation or self-love you will have a mess on your hands. Whether you are single or married if you don't know who you are you will live most of the time in a state of depression, anger, anxiety or sadness because you're so disempowered looking for the external world to make you happy and give you your value.

So ask yourself, "Where am I in relationship to my Self? What choices do I make daily that give off a resounding *I'm valuable?* Do I participate in life in a way that mirrors my value or do I feel I must give myself away to gain acceptance, love and safety?" Very often when you are seeking outside validation, you're giving off energy of weakness and neediness that ironically will produce a response confirming your biggest fear, that you aren't valuable.

Have you ever had someone try too hard to be your friend

or lover? What was your response? They may have been a very nice person but their neediness made you feel uncomfortable and so you probably ended up avoiding or ignoring them. When you expect someone else to give you your value, they often feel so much pressure they turn off or they feel superior and the relationship becomes dysfunctional.

If you're in a relationship and look to your partner to give you your value it's hurting your partnership. If you don't value yourself you are sucking from the other person. Ask yourself, "What am I bringing to the table?" How do they know how to value you if you don't know how to value you? So many women feel guilty at the thought of empowering themselves. They're fearful they won't be loved any more. Good guilt is when you smack your kid and feel bad. False guilt is when you know you haven't done anything wrong yet you still feel guilty because of your conditioning. This kind of guilt wears you down. If you aren't sure whether it's false guilt ask a good friend—they'll tell you the truth. If it is you need to let it go. Inspire yourself with the knowing that when you value yourself you are a more equal partner. Can you see how you actually feed your fears when you don't know who you are?

I coached a woman, Carol, who was the ultimate people pleaser, always showing up with gifts and paying for everyone. One time she was at a conference and was asked to get lunch menus for her instructor. She happily went out and instead of gathering menus decided to buy several salads, feeling confident her teacher would like one of them. The teacher turned out to be very hard to please; not only did she not care for any of the salads, she admonished Carol for not following instructions. This sent Carol into a tailspin, feeling like a failure. Not getting the approval she expected she became resentful and blaming.

Through some coaching she realized the underlying motivation for her pattern of over-giving was to be liked and loved, and to feel important and valued. This awareness helped her let go of her reaction and start to make some changes in other areas. The next time she was faced with a situation where she would have normally paid for her friends, she sat back and did not offer. Little by little she shifted her people-pleasing behavior and was pleasantly surprised to find she did not lose love and felt more authentic in how she showed up.

Can you think of actions you've taken that were off? Where you perhaps sought validation, approval and confirmation that you were worthy of being loved? Reflect on what you could do to course correct. Is there a boundary you could have set or something you could have said that would have allowed you to own your value?

Constantly seeking external validation, it's no wonder over time the poor body starts to break down from the stress and the mind becomes frazzled. Now, dear heart, are you ready to stop the madness?

It's time to delve into your Divine essence. When you don't know who you are, it's nearly impossible for your brilliance to find its way out. But I know, because you're reading this book, you are ready to set yourself free! Start by taking a moment to reflect on how you go about gaining approval so you can escape that prison. Is it by over-giving, being a good girl, relying on your beauty, sexuality, doing for others, accomplishments?

Isn't it worth doing the sleuthing now so you can live *la dolce vita* forever more? I know you can do it, and more importantly, you deserve it!

How do you stop the madness and take your power back?

What you need to do is take baby steps that honor you. By doing this you'll build confidence and respect. The fear that others won't like/love you if you don't cater to their needs has got to go! There is usually no truth to this—it's just a false belief you've convinced yourself is real. On the other hand, if someone does pull away from you for standing in your power, know this was not an association that served your best interest and trust new doors will open for more favorable relationships.

Another benefit to loving you is that you'll stop taking personally what others say. You may not like what they say, but you will discern if there is truth to it or not, without having a knee-jerk reaction. If there is truth to it, you will have the maturity to acknowledge it and choose to change or not. You'll also start to set appropriate boundaries that make you feel empowered, resulting in respect. When you know who you are, you don't need anyone to approve of you because YOU approve of you. This ignites your diamond power!

Reviving the Feminine

Do you live primarily in your masculine mode always striving to prove your worth? Are you goal oriented living your entire day "doing"? Look at how you may have abandoned your feminine. Be honest and check your behavior—are you aggressive, rigid, strongly opinionated, controlling, snitty and snarky with a need to always be right?

I have to admit my persona was peppered with all of those pesky traits when I was married. Worse yet, I was clueless that I'd buried my feminine. Somehow I had stepped out of my stilettos and into man boots fully believing I was doing the right thing and saving the day.

Fortunately like all things in life, when we are severely off track we get slapped in the face to snap out of it. I'll never forget receiving a birthday present from my ex shortly after we had separated. He was known for his good taste so I was looking forward to opening his gift. However, what I saw when I unwrapped it, a pair of Prada loafers that could have doubled for Michelin tires, I screamed and threw them across the room. I almost clipped my friend's ears as they flew through the air. Jon picked one up and laughed as I cried from the deepest part of my soul. It wasn't the gift that upset me as much as it was what it represented. This was a man's shoe—rubbery, black and practical—ugh! Where was the feminine strappy sandal? Was this what he thought of me? Was this how I presented to the world? What a wake-up call.

I was angry with my ex but mostly with me—how had I lost myself without even knowing? And, how could I have fooled myself so completely to believe just because I'm a woman I'm feminine? The pursuit of material success had blinded me to my manly behavior. It was shocking to realize I had been living just as big of a lie as my ex was with his cheating escapades.

Once I got to this point I had to keep digging to uncover the truth—and that's what you'll need to do too if you want to find your way home. Brutal honesty is necessary to clearly see what's been driving your behavior—what's the underlying motivation. Whether you're seeking external approval or have become a shim (woman acting as a man), most women are motivated to satisfy the core need to feel valuable, safe and loved. It's true, my valiant efforts were rooted in wanting to feel all of those things, but I also wanted to feel powerful. Since I was not empowered in knowing who I was, and in my mind it wasn't enough or safe just to be me, I sought power as I saw power—belonging to men. Being powerful meant emulating a man's behavior. When I grew up there were very few role models of powerful women who embodied the feminine. This is an unfortunate reality of our culture.

A few years ago I was at a book-marketing seminar and had lunch with a beautiful Japanese woman. She was elegantly dressed and had a very graceful yet powerful presence. We spoke about the epidemic of women embracing their masculine side in the United States and she said it wasn't our fault. In Japan women were raised with courses on how to be in their feminine power. She said the businesswomen of Japan know how to flip to feminine at the appropriate times and the American women were never taught.

If you are pursuing the masculine route of accomplishing with a forceful energy and independence, as I did, are you finding life lonely?

I recently had a conversation with a client in her late 40s. She shared that she and several of her female friends who had pursued careers and independence are now regretful and sad about the choices they made to climb the corporate ladder. If she had it to do over again, she said, she would have chosen more balance in her life.

To further that sentiment, there have been a lot of studies on women across the board. Findings show that the more accomplished they are, the less happy. Many of them say they sacrificed too much and have much regret. There is so much confusion about accomplishment because even though women are able to participate in running the world they aren't happy. As a matter of fact, it seems happiness levels are declining every year.

What I believe is waking up in many women today is the

desire to reconnect with who they are and to be all that they can be. This means understanding that everyone possesses both masculine and feminine energy. The trick is to balance the yin and the yang

Don't get me wrong; you need the masculine to make things happen. But when we focus on accomplishing for the sake of accomplishing it's very difficult to create a fulfilling life. On the other hand solely living in the feminine will have you coming up with fantastic ideas that never get implemented. The feminine definitely needs the masculine mojo to give legs to her creative concepts and give her the ambition to get out of bed every day and take them to the world. You need to find a balance between the two because you need them both.

Although the women's movement of the '60s and '70s sent our feminine scurrying in many ways, let's look at the positive side: we gained a lot of ground. We don't want to throw that away, we just need to tame it and swing the pendulum back to balance the two.

Take a minute and reflect on the masculine and feminine traits mentioned in Chapter 2. Which ones resonate with you? What comes up for you? Did you experience any discomfort with either? Notice if there's anything you don't trust or what judgments you have about the masculine and the feminine.

One of my clients, Jacqueline, thought the feminine was weak and ineffective so she disrespected feminine energy. She was living primarily in her masculine. She had to look at what her payoff was and what the cost had been to her life. Her payoff was to be in control yet for years she butt heads with her husband. If you favor one over the other ask yourself the same questions. What is the payoff and what is the cost?

Possessing masculine power was never the gold at the end

of the rainbow. Stepping into it was a way for us to get our foot in the door and let our talents and brilliance be heard, contributing to the well-being of the planet. It was never meant to disconnect us from who we are. Embracing your feminine will bring back balance, instilling peace and genuine happiness.

One of my clients, Deanna, really took this message to heart. She joined my playshop because she felt she had lost her luster and her marriage of 25 years needed a little rekindling. She felt responsible as she had been steeped in her masculine side and tended to be negative more often than not. She knew this wasn't helping her marriage or the other relationships in her life.

One of the course assignments involved creating a Romance-Capade with your own twists and turns. Determined to contribute to her relationship in a fun-filled way, Deanna took this on with a passion and together we designed a night to remember for her and her husband.

The plan was for them to celebrate their anniversary at a cozy bed and breakfast out of town. She wanted to do something special that would intrigue her man and re-ignite the passion in their marriage. We schemed up a plan for her to excuse herself at dinner, find the waiter, and give him a wrapped gift to give to her hubby when he brought dessert.

Needless to say, her husband was all smiles when he opened her surprise treat—a pair of naughty dice with a suggestive note! Minutes later they were rushing to their hotel room with excitement and anticipation. They danced and laughed and had a hot time with the dice. Since it was winter on the East Coast, they ended this magical evening toasting champagne glasses in a bubble bath while watching the snow blanket the city.

Deanna called me when she returned home, absolutely ecstatic, saying it was the most romantic night they had ever had and her husband LOVED it. She felt completely empowered, happy, and confident—and ready to plan another.

Moving from Outer to Inner Validation

The wondrous women of today would make sizzling shifts if they let go of the belief that doing for others, accomplishments, and somebody else's definition of beauty gives us worth and instead embrace the knowing that just in our beautiful BEING we are valuable. We don't have to DO anything to prove our merit.

To do this you have to recognize that there is nothing wrong with you and that you are safe and always loved by God/The Divine/Source or whatever your belief system may be. Even though many women are haunted by childhood beliefs and experiences that cause anxiety about who they need to be or how they need to act in order to be safe and loved, the reality is they are now adults, fully in charge of their life. Whatever motivated your behavior as a child doesn't need to continue motivating your behavior as an adult. Get current with who you are today and replace the old way of thinking with an updated way of thinking that honors and speaks to your inherent diamond essence. When you develop Self-love your light will shine in a most magnificent way.

Jolene is a great example of a woman who learned that knowing who she is has a lot to do with self-love and acceptance. Trying to find an outfit she felt good in to meet a date for dinner she became frustrated with what she called her "chunky monkey hips and thighs." None of us can relate to that, right? Oy! In the process she tried on and rejected just about everything in her closet causing her room to look like a bomb hit it. As she put on one of her last options, a skirt that hugged her hips more than she liked, she realized she was running out of choices. She decided she could either leave the house feeling fat and ugly or embrace her voluptuous curves. She wisely chose to see herself as a beautiful full-figured woman with a lot of vavoom!

As she entered the restaurant she silently repeated to herself, "I am a beautiful, sexy woman" swinging her hips proudly. Needless to say, her attitude created a whirlwind of attractive energy. Several male heads turned and craned to look as she sashayed through the café with confidence and sensuality. Her date had been watching this scenario with pleasure and greeted her with a big smile, proud to be having dinner with such a sexy and desired woman. She was surprised but delighted to see that others' acceptance of her depended on and mirrored her own acceptance.

Are you still weighing yourself down with self-judgments and self-sabotage? Check in with yourself by asking, "Is my old way of doing and thinking creating the life I want?" I'm going to guess your answer is no, otherwise you wouldn't be reading this book.

Over time your patterns have become ingrained habits, but the good news is you can break them and create powerful new patterns that align with the truth of who you are. If you want to form new patterns try this:

1) Sit with your ankles crossed and your wrists crossed, palms facing each other and hands interlocked and close your eyes.

2) Take some deep breaths.

3) Become your biggest fan. Affirm you are all the things you've wanted to hear from other people—say, "I am beautiful, worthy/valuable, special" until you feel a shift, emotionally, physically or mentally.

4) Regardless who you've given your power away to, take it back by declaring, "I am the only person who gets to decide that I'm enough, that I'm worthy and that I'm valuable." Go ahead, repeat this and see how you feel. Is there a burst of energy shooting through your body? Is there a sense of empowerment? Do you feel stronger and more confident? Can you feel your body relaxing, your anxiety waning and your need for external approval fading? Welcome home!

The greatest gift you'll experience when going from seeking outside validation to providing it for yourself is a huge sense of peace and well-being. The best way to make this shift is to start making choices that will reflect back to your own value. And more importantly, when you do make a choice, show up for yourself! If you decide to nurture yourself by going for a run and a friend calls to vent, either let the call go to voicemail or tell her you'll phone her later. When you allow others' needs to take precedence over your own, you are not valuing yourself. Make yourself the priority and stop the guilt by reminding yourself when you feel frazzled, the mean team usually shows up and that's not good for anyone! So take a break. It will help you keep your stress down, improve your health, and allow you to be even more nurturing to others.

Everyone gets a role in life starting with your birth order. This extends to your friends and co-workers and romantic partnerships. You may not like it but people put you in that box. And when you are known for this your ego makes sure you live up to it. If you want to change this labeling you will have to be firmly committed because the people around you probably won't like it. They want to keep you in that role—they are used to you this way and won't easily accept your new persona. Especially if it's an empowering one! However, if you value yourself you will make the change and not let other people affect your choice.

To be in alignment with your authentic Self is a state you want to strive to achieve, not something you experience here and there. So become your best friend, and treat yourself and others with consistent, positive and loving action.

The more women I coach and talk with the more I realize the need to set boundaries is HUGE! Are you sacrificing your needs to accommodate everyone else? If you want 30 minutes to yourself to decompress from a hectic day, take it! If you know calling a friend will help you lighten up, call! If you want healthy food but your partner won't eat it—buy it! If you want to go to yoga....go! Why? Because when Mama's happy, everybody is happy! You're a better partner when you take care of yourself.

When you accept and love yourself, have appreciation for you and remember who you are, something beautiful begins to happen—you sparkle from the inside out and start attracting and manifesting all the good things in life. It's like catching a ride on a magic carpet.

Pause and Reflect

1) Do you allow other people's opinions and beliefs to affect how you see yourself? Set at least one new boundary with someone close to you this week.

2) Do you live more in your "doing" or "being" state? What can you do to balance these two energies?

3) What motivates you to do things for other people? Is it to look good? To be liked/loved? Approved of? Is it to satisfy your need to feel valuable? Is it because it brings you true joy?

4) What three things can you do right now that would exemplify and show the world you are owning who you are?

5) Set aside 10 minutes a day to meditate/pray and ask, "Who am I?" Listen for the answers from above and journal the insights and revelations until you are able to love Self and know this is the real you.

Revel in Your Radiance

Do something to feed your feminine essence every day. Create celebration for who you are as a woman. You may choose to honor yourself in any of the following ways or come up with your own jollification:

1) Dance—put on your favorite song and do a triumphant dance. Let your hips sway and revel in the joy of being a woman.
2) Applaud—clap and raise your arms to the heavens, letting

out a huge wooohooo.
3) Flowers—romance yourself with your favorite flower. Inhale the fragrance deeply, letting it fill every part of your body, connecting you with your delicate, beautiful nature.
4) Lotion with love—if you've spent your day in action take a few minutes before you slip into bed to lotion your body with loving caresses. Choose something lovely like lavender or put a drop of jasmine or ylang ylang into your favorite lotion.
5) Eat or drink something that makes you feel decadent, delicious and honored.
6) Wear something pink—this is the color of unconditional love. Adorning yourself in this feminine hue will be like wrapping yourself in bliss.
7) Put on a pretty nighty or lingerie—slip into something satin and silky or diaphanous and flowing. Touch the fabric and let the sensation flow through your body.
8) Listen to romantic music.
9) Dab an essential oil like joy or ylang ylang on your ankles and wrists and in your cleavage—the scent will make you feel delicious.

Chapter 9

L...Laugh and Play

How long has it been since you had a good laugh? I mean a gut wrenching, tears streaming, cheeks hurting kind of laugh. Well? Be honest. Did you know the average person used to laugh 20 minutes a day and now it's less than 5 minutes? Isn't that sad? When did we all get so serious? It's clear we've forgotten how to play! That's a crying shame because laughter is not only the sunshine of the soul, it creates instant intimacy and connection, which is what you want, right?

Laughter and playfulness lead to a more joyful state of being. As Oscar Wilde put it, "An inordinate amount of pleasure is the secret of remaining young." Who doesn't want to be around someone who is youthful and happy? It also keeps you present. Most of us spend the majority of our time in the past or in the future, keeping us separate and isolated. In order to connect we have to be present. Another plus, whatever you say when you are light and playful is much more likely to be heard and received, creating open and honest communication.

You don't want to turn into one of those snappy, cranky, controlling women over 40, do you? I was recently at a seminar and asked a woman her opinion on the title of a workshop I was planning. She growled back at me that she didn't have her hormones and could care less about sparkling. I had to step back to steer clear of the venom.

Get off the control train, stop with the stubbornness, release your rigidity—these trolls will imprison you. As a woman you have an innate gift of flirtatiousness, playfulness, and softness. You may have lost touch with it but this is your feminine power, so reconnect with it and work it, girl!

Opening up to playfulness gives you the greatest gift—it frees the creative expression of your soul. Suddenly your charisma, magnetic charm, and vibrancy are larger than life. This is your diamond essence, that lively glow that money can't buy. Viva la Diamond Power!

Get ready to step outside of your routine to make fun and pleasure a priority. If you don't know how or where to begin, this chapter is for you. This step of the SPARKLE System will inspire you to unleash your playful feminine spirit—that juicy part of you that's been buried far too long and is *dyyy-ing* to be discovered.

Make Time for Playtime

Once I had a last minute offer to take a belly dancing class and found myself coming up with all sorts of reasons why it wasn't the right time for me to go. Finally I stopped and said to myself, "Sherri, you've always wanted to take belly dancing—be spontaneous and get movin' girl." In other words, seize the day!

This is what I teach for heaven's sake—live in the moment... have fun...do what makes you happy...step outside the box... embrace your passion. Yet here I was fighting my own advice. So I want to say, I understand when you resist and put pleasure on the back burner—it's the first instinct, especially when you've got a to-do list a mile long. It's so seductive to pen those delicious check off's—I really do understand.

But I'm here to tell you, living a life of "have to's" with few or no "get to's" will leave you feeling unfulfilled, bored, or disconnected and pull your energy down, making you less attractive and creating the opposite of what you want. When you start having fun you will activate your inner sparkle and this in-love-with-life attitude will make you irresistible to the opposite sex. Make a conscious choice to reclaim your playful spirit.

Don't make it hard! The simplest things can bring a whole lot of joy. One of my clients, Jody, did something so simple it was genius and brought back the carefree days of youth. Remember those bottles of bubbles? Well, she bought a bunch and kept them on her dining room table. When she had dinner parties her guests were invited to start blowing bubbles—they had contests to see who could blow the biggest bubbles, blow them the highest, blow them into clusters. In short, they had a blast and it set the mood for a very playful evening.

Adopting an open mind proved to be the Holy Grail of inventiveness for me, leading to *a lot* of laughter and an abundance of good times. Not surprisingly, the more I was laughing the more I was sparkling, and the more fabulous things started happening both personally and professionally. Creative ideas were going off like Jiffy Pop in my mind and guess what? Not only did I start seeing myself in a new light, I was excited about my life again. I felt a freedom like never before, and *so will you.*

Back to the belly dancing opportunity. Turns out it was so much fun I stayed for the next class...burlesque! Allowing myself to live in the moment and try something I had always wanted to do gave me the chance to express my feminine creative Self and it felt so fantastic I didn't want to leave. I thought back to my indecision and excuses and realized it was my stealth committee working to keep my nose to the grind, away from joy, in a safe little box.

So abandon your list, turn off the "sensible" voice, stop listening to the gremlins and free yourself to have fun. Live in the present moment and mix things up. Trust me, that check-off list isn't going anywhere. The next time you have a choice between getting something done or getting playful, flip to fun—you will be glad you did!

9 Benefits to Having Fun

Understanding why it's important to have fun seems like a no-brainer, but if women were so clear about it why do they put it on the back burner, dismissing it as though it's taboo, a luxury or reserved for kids? The truth is, most of us have forgotten the delicious gifts of playing.

When I started dating after my divorce I got involved with a man whose energy mixed with mine in a way that brought out my creative playful spirit. I found there were nine brilliant benefits I experienced just by having fun. Incidentally, these were not exclusive to me. My married friends and clients also mentioned these wondrous windfalls when they gave themselves permission to play—it's universal.

1) Really Radiant—The first thing I noticed was playfulness and pleasure made my skin shine. It's a glow that some women try to achieve with make-up, even plastic surgery, but the radiance that I'm talking about is the kind that comes from the inside out—making your eyes sparkle and your face glow. It creates beauty in women of ALL ages. Laughter helps to expand your blood vessels, increasing your blood flow and this gives you radiance.

2) Full of Femininity—When you are playful you are more in tune with your feminine nature. Any walls of control come tumbling down, giving you an inviting, approachable attitude that is perfect for intimacy and connection. You feel freer to indulge in flirty behavior—putting you in touch with your feminine essence.

3) Healthy Help—Laughing is like the healthiest drink you can imagine on steroids. Tons of hormones and chemicals are released that have an amazingly positive effect on the body—successfully lifting depression, sadness, anxiety and plenty of other emotional culprits. So the next time you're feeling blue call a friend who will make you laugh, tune into America's funniest videos, go to laughter yoga (www.laughteryoga.org) and get your sparkle back!

4) Man-Opener—Let's face it, most women are a bit chattier than men and often complain their guys don't communicate and share as much as they'd like. Hallelujah girlfriends, you'll be thrilled to know laughing will open them up! Despite the fact that men inherently speak a fraction of the words in a day

that women do, if they are relaxed and enjoying themselves they not only talk more, they become more vulnerable about what they share.

5) Confidence Creator—There is no room for fear when you are laughing and having fun. Letting go of your inhibitions and insecurities gives you the courage to be YOU. This alignment makes you feel good about yourself and whenever you feel good about yourself you are building confidence and self-esteem. When surveyed, men rated authentic confidence as ultra-sexy.

6) Fresh Perspective—The minute you start having fun you open to inspiration and will notice new solutions surfacing. A great way to fast track to a fresh perspective is traveling. Whether you plan a weekend getaway with your lover or hit the highway for a fun girls trip, getting out of town will generate new insights that will bring you peace and happiness.

7) Creates Connection—We women LOVE to connect and nothing makes that happen quicker than engaging in some playtime, whether it's with your man or a girlfriend! Single or married when you are light and laughing you are opening your heart center where connection happens. An easy way to connect is a simple smile. Did you know smiling, in the land of body language, is the #1 thing you can do to invite a man into your space? Start smiling now because it sends a signal to men that it's safe to approach.

8) Instant Intimacy—When you share a good time with someone it creates a bond of intimacy. This type of intimacy is authentic—it's real and lasting. So make sure your playground is open and active!

9) Lasting Love—When you are connected and you are

experiencing genuine intimacy your heart opens and expands. You may find yourself falling in love, rekindling your love, or growing the love you already have. It's impossible not to. When you laugh with someone they become a cherished part of your heart.

Voilá the benefits of having fun. So now wouldn't you agree it's worth making playtime a daily habit?

Here's what you need to watch out for. If your life or relationship isn't going the way you want, it's understandably disappointing and so tempting to withdraw or slip into separation. I know, I've been there! After my divorce I fell deeply in love and when that didn't work out I was miserable for a very long time, disconnecting, isolating, blaming, and punishing myself. Daily fun kinda went by the wayside and I had some big ole pity parties.

But here's what I finally got—it was solely up to me to turn my life around again and get back to those things that made me feel happy and alive. I was wasting my life wallowing from disappointment and that's when I began to understand the benefits in a different light. Until you are intimate, connected and in love with *you*, you'll live life like you're watching a movie—never a part of things, never starring in your own life. And if you're in a relationship it will never have the depth you want or last in the way that you want until you own it, personally.

When I had this awakening I started living again—spending my free time going on weekend adventures with friends and venturing back into dating. I got back to me—and now when things flip around I have my handy Revitalize My Vibrancy Emergency List (when you Pause and Reflect at the end of the chapter you will have the opportunity to create your own) that gives me a number of options to get me laughing and feeling good again. It's definitely a process and I'm always learning, just like you.

However, I don't want you to be in the remedial program like I was—I want you to soar. If you commit to having FUN, living with passion, seeking silliness, and experiencing life with a thirst, you will be guaranteed a happy life where you'll be irresistible to men, in fact to everyone—and you will draw to you every dream your heart desires.

The Art of Flirting

What's the juiciest, most natural expression of feminine playfulness? *Flirting*, of course! Wikipedia defines it as "playful behavior intended to arouse sexual interest," but holy Toledo, it's so much more than that. It's not just about getting a guy's attention; it's about the sheer enjoyment of being connected to your sensuality and feminine essence.

Whether you are charming someone you've just met, cooing at a baby, relishing the caress of the wind on your cheeks, playing with your dog, or teasing your partner out of a potential blow up—it all falls under flirty fun, which is largely based on your desire to live a life of pleasure. Best of all, whenever you embrace this vivacious behavior, whatever you wish for comes to you more smoothly. It's a natural mood lightener. Simple, yet powerful.

The big "get" is when you approach things in a fun way you feel light and your nervousness disappears. No matter the outcome you are relaxed and able to absorb and receive it without feeling embarrassed or ashamed. Like a duck you let it roll off your back knowing you took a chance—a chance that most would not. Because of this you feel *fan-tas-tic* and very proud. Get your deliciousness on and start playing—your confidence will soar!

Okay, having peeked at the power of playfulness, it's time to ask how's your flirt factor? I have to confess, mine stunk! I didn't want the attention so I never learned the art. But after my divorce I knew I had to do some developing in this area—even if it was just to remind myself to make eye contact and smile. Seems so easy but this was huge for me.

How about you? How do you rank on the flirt-o-meter? Have you mastered your "come-hither" or are you on the bashful side? If you're already a fabulous flirt, kudos! But what's a shy girl to do?

Try calling in your most savvy femme fatale friends and learn a trick or two. That's what I did. Yes, indeed, I learned quite a few titillating tactics, which I share with you below. My suggestion is to pick your poison (these are lethal moves—the poor guy won't know what hit him), practice where appropriate so that you'll start to own it, and then go have some fun!

First of all it's important to be aware that men are visual, so it makes sense to use mannerisms and actions that play into this. Creating a "stir" was a big tip—who knew all it takes is a little calculated movement to rile him up and connect you with your feminine power?

Try these simple actions:

- Crossing and uncrossing your legs.
- Getting up to use the ladies room (whether you need to or not) just to cause some commotion with your slow, sultry walk.

- Wearing a jacket (even if you don't need one) so you can shimmy out of it during conversation to draw attention to your beautiful essence.

Here are some more man magnets. They may seem trite but they're killer, especially in combination. Choose a body movement and add eye contact.

- Dangle your shoe from your toe.
- Look at your guy a second longer than is considered appropriate.
- Lick your lips.
- Touch his hand, forearm, leg, small of back.
- Circle the rim of your glass with your fingertip while looking at him.
- Eat with pleasure and lick your fingers.
- Look at your man, then look down, then look back a few more times.
- Tilt your head to one side, baring your throat.
- Touch or fondle your neck or necklace.
- Sitting Pretty—the sexiest sitting position for women, bar none, is the leg twine, highlighting the muscle tone of your legs.

What's in a Face?

Even though your face makes up less than 5% of the body surface, it is the canvas of your personality, image and sensuality. If you're cringing, stop! Instead, rejoice—a face doesn't have to be drop-dead gorgeous to attract the opposite sex. Every face has its own visual appeal, especially when you add playfulness, humor, and a feminine flirt.

As a matter of fact, the most interesting faces have idiosyncratic "signature" traits like Tom Cruise's boyish grin or Elvis Presley's upper lip curl that gave him a "bad-boy" look. What about Julia Roberts' mega-watt smile or Lucille Ball's comic facial language? The facial expressions and personality of these famous faces make them memorable, not perfect features and symmetry.

After 40 many women start to worry about their attractiveness and desirability. But here's a fact you'll love: research in social psychology shows that men find *expressive* faces far more attractive and appealing than beautiful ones. That's right, facial movements are considered to be more beguiling than the features themselves. Doesn't that take the edge off of aging? All you have to do is let your personality and inner sparkle express itself through your eyes and smile and you become ageless. Regardless what you look like, light up your face with expressive lips, eyelids, and brow motion. *Voilà* the fountain of youth!

Smiling lights you up from the inside out. No matter what you look like, flashing your pearly whites will always make you sparkle and your eyes twinkle. And it's the quickest way to communicate your joy, happiness, love, friendliness, and approachability.

On the flirtatious side, a smile is equivalent to a feminine lair—inviting a man into your space. Universally, your smile has the ability to turn somebody's day around. How incredible is that? Why not make it a part of your day, every day, and you'll instantly see changes that you will love.

Think about Dolly Parton—she is a natural flirt and oozes femininity. She says some pretty sexy things and they always come out fun and flirty because of her big smile, mischievous eyes, and bright attitude.

And remember Princess Diana's famous flirting? She would look down and then cock her head to the side and look up with playful eyes and a killer smile—charming everyone in sight and the world at large. *She* had it going on and so can YOU!

Next time you are out and about or on a date night make sure you are fully facially expressed to amplify your gorgeous goddess essence.

Seduction & Sensuality

The art of seduction is all about creating the anticipation of pleasure without saying a word...and the secret to do this is that you must know pleasure before you can give pleasure.

Use your body language by creating curves with your stance, uncross your arms, and show your vulnerability and softness by exposing your throat.

Let your hand trail from the side of your face and down your throat to create allure and interest. And touch those thighs and arms with love when you're sitting—women who caress their bodies captivate men.

The best way to connect with your sensuality is to *dance!* Whether it's doing the tango and dancing cheek to cheek with your lover, getting down with Barry White on the tabletops of your home, or some steamy pole dancing at the S Factor, there is no better way to express your Self than to move those hips and shimmy down.

One of my clients, Leslie, was feeling disconnected from her femininity and sensuality, feeling rather invisible to men. We decided dance would be a good exercise for her so she started taking some classes at her gym that appealed to her. Just swaying sensually immediately made her feel more in touch with her body and her feminine essence. The more she danced the more she opened up and the next time I saw her she looked radiant—REALLY happy.

And the icing on the cake? Guys started asking her out more frequently because she was living in her femininity—emanating her *vixen vibe*. So get out there on the dance floor and start celebrating your sexy self!

Frisky Frolics

When's the last time you put on a wig and did a jig with your sweetheart? This may sound crazy but you have to admit, it's pretty playful.

If the boudoir has gotten boring and you want a rockin' relationship, you'll need to "mix things up" to keep it interesting, fresh, fun and adventuresome. Laughing and playing are the key elements to emotional intimacy, helping you build that rock solid relationship you crave. Making the time to be playmates is super important. Relationship expert Dr. David Schnarch says successful relationships laugh and play, so take some risks and dare to be wild. Let your inner child out. Be silly, wacky, laugh like a hyena. Allow yourself the freedom to be totally uninhibited and you'll start to feel young and alive.

One of my clients, Marlene, got very playful and creative to spice things up in her marriage. She decided to go camping with her honey...in her living room. As she got more and more into the planning she found her creative expression pouring out, helping her add her own sensual twists and turns. She pitched a tent in front of the fireplace, kept the room dark except for the light from the fireplace and a couple of lanterns, fixed some great camp-side finger foods, and even found a night sounds CD to emulate the woods and a running stream. Not only was Marlene's hubby totally impressed with her creativity, he saw a different side to her that reignited his passion and deepened his love for her. Seeing her happy made him happy, bringing their connection to a whole new level. Creating a different atmosphere within your own home is a creative, fun, inexpensive way to get out of a romantic rut and breathe newness into your relationship—check out the Romance-Capades in the Passport to Passion section of this book for ideas.

Another client, Tory, was a little sad that her first trip to Paris, the city of love, would be for business and not for pleasure. Understandably she wanted to share this special place with her husband. We talked about it and came up with a brilliant plan—a sexy adventure she would bring back to him. While she was there she gathered menus, wine, and other fun accoutrements. When she got home she re-created a sizzling night in a French bistro. She had the time of her life planning this interlude in Paris; engaging waiters to teach her some playful French phrases and shop owners to adorn her in luscious lingerie. It made her trip fabulously fun, and the return all the sweeter. Her man was blown away and became very supportive of ALL her business travel!

My client Olga makes me smile every time I think of her. Well into her 60s and a mother of six, she is full of fun and still embraces her feminine flirty spirit. She and her husband planned a trip to visit their kids. They decided she would fly a week early to help out with one of their daughters who had a health challenge, and he would drive so they would have a car. After 45 years of marriage Olga was pining for her partner, missing him terribly. We talked about what she could do to surprise him when he arrived. We decided on a "Giddy-Up" theme and boy, did we have a blast putting it together!

We got a red lace panty from Victoria's Secret and attached a sexy note telling him to "find the filly that fits into these!" After a Hi-Ho Silver sign-off, she put the sizzling surprise on the pillow of their bed with excited anticipation and then went to dinner with her girls. When he arrived later that night he was tired from his three-day cross-country drive, but you better believe after finding the lingerie he was on the phone immediately telling her to get home pronto!

I love this story for so many reasons, but mainly because it exemplifies no matter how old you are or how many years you and your mate have been together, unleashing your playful, sexy side will keep the flames of passion soaring.

The last step in the SPARKLE System is perhaps the most delicious of all. Embrace your life with love and joy!

Pause and Reflect

1) Conjure up a list of things you and your man, or you and a friend, would have a blast doing...like salsa dancing, laughter yoga, a Moroccan cooking class, or an art exhibit. Every week, select one and do it!

2) Pick a Romance-Capade from the Passport to Passion section of this book that sounds like fun. Will it thrill your man too? Start planning! Call on your gal pals to help you create a romantic adventure to remember.

3) Create your own Revitalize My Vibrancy Emergency List. Write down at least 10 things you can do to bring a smile back to your face and heart. This may include a run or walk in nature, chatting with a friend who makes you laugh, listening to a guided meditation, prayer, getting a massage or counting your blessings—it doesn't matter what your list contains, it only matters that they are actions you can take to feel vibrant and alive again.

Revel in Your Radiance

Whether you are single or committed, reconnect with the lost art of flirting and feel your femininity explode. When you engage in this purely pleasurable activity, watch how walls crumble and openings are created, not only inviting him into your space making him feel safe and excited to step closer but bringing more joy and happiness to your life in every way. Flirt with life! Being grounded in your playful sensual Self will draw men in like honey. It's the masculine/feminine law of polarity in full force. Rock it, you delicious damsel!

Chapter 9

E...Embrace Your Life

Now that you've dusted off your diamond and fallen in love with yourself, you're free to embrace your feminine power and live life fully! If you think about it, did it ever serve you to hold back? No way! So get involved with all those delicious opportunities and adventures waiting for you. It will bring an explosion of happiness to your soul—and make you even more irresistible.

Let's recap. Moving through the SPARKLE steps, you've gotten clarity on your dreams, identified the sludge holding you back, pinpointed your passions, connected to your leading lady attitude, renewed your relationship with you, remembered who you *really* are, and put playtime on your planner because, baby, you were born to be wild!

Now it's time to culminate what you've learned and fully embrace your life with passion and joy. Right now you might have zero excitement for your day; it's more an obligation than a life. But imagine waking up with a genuine, "I can't wait to start my day" kind of excitement. Put this vibration out into the world and your life will change, guaranteed.

All it takes is looking at each day *as if* you're on vacation. That's right—this step of the SPARKLE system actually encourages you to work less, love more, step outside your comfort zone, make fun a priority, and expect great things to happen. When you couple these actions with the power of appreciation and gratitude, you will become quite the radiant goddess, riding the flow of Divine consciousness. Everything becomes brighter, more vivid, more colorful.

It's been scientifically proven that we attract what we put out. So embrace life with zest and zeal and the most outrageous things will begin to happen. Unlimited abundance. Magic. Plan to pinch yourself daily while shouting, "I LOVE my life!" Ahhh, bliss!

Live Life as if You're on Vacation

Why not wake up and approach the day as though you're on holiday? Think about how open and carefree you feel on vacation—it's heaven! You tingle in anticipation of the new things you'll see, the adventures you'll have, the quality time you'll spend with your loved ones, the rest and relaxation you'll have *at last*. There are new friends to be made, new foods to be savored and new experiences to be had. Life outside your normal routine thrills your spirit and fills your body with excitement—you can practically taste the wonderful times ahead.

Embracing life is about greeting each day with this same

enthusiasm. *Expect* to have fun, *expect* things to go well for you, *expect* to see and do things that delight you.

I know what you're thinking: who has time to dream about vacations? With everything you've got on your plate, your mind is overwhelmed and you barely have time to eat or bathe or sleep. But the truth is, if you can conjure the *feeling* of being on holiday your mind doesn't know the difference; it will help you attract glorious situations and outcomes to your day just because of that shift in energy.

If you find this prospect challenging, pull out your favorite travel picture and put it where you will see it first thing in the morning. Gaze at the photo as long as necessary to recall the good times and feel yourself filling up with positive memories.

It doesn't take much to put you in a sunny mood. For example, this morning I went to Starbucks to get my vanilla/hazelnut latte before settling into my day of writing. As I got out of my car I heard the idling of a motor. In the here and now it was just a truck in a parking lot, but the sound transported me to a delicious memory of being in a Turkish sea port on a gorgeous morning drinking coffee with friends on a private sail boat, smelling the mixture of engine oil and salty air, excited to see what adventures the day would bring.

Hours later I still have that same giddiness inside of me. I feel like a kid on Christmas morning viewing everything my eyes land upon as the most amazing gift. Suddenly I'm in touch with all of my senses! I'm sniffing the air for lovely scents, listening to the birds sing, feeling the sun on my face, taking in the liveliness of the people and the promise of the day.

Starting your day with the same excitement you have on vacation will set you up to experience life's treasures. When you get up ask yourself, "What new experience will I create today? What will I see? What will I do and feel that will add to my enjoyment of life?" Then have an appreciation for whatever shows up in your day—how can you learn from it, grow from it, evolve? Make this simple shift in perception and watch your life magically transform!

Work Less

A no-brainer? Unfortunately not for everyone. Some of you do-divas may need formal instruction to cut back on your workload if you want to enjoy a more balanced and happy life. Whether you are a mom, a dedicated employee, an entrepreneur, or all three, give yourself permission to Do less and Be more. It's always easier to intellectualize than integrate new learning, but I'm here to tell you your life *will not change* until you ditch the old way of being and step into a new paradigm. Ask yourself, "If not now, when?"

Instead of shelving this section "for later," keep the momentum going by creating a "Joie de Vivre list" of 100 experiences you would love to have before you leave this planet. Your list should include anything and everything you have even the tiniest hankering to try. It can be something as simple as spending more time with your child to sampling the best chocolates of the world to writing a book to belly dancing to sitting in a pyramid to riding an elephant to hang gliding in Bavaria to learning how to walk with a sexy saunter on a tight rope!

Really stretch your imagination to allow for the outrageous, but don't forget the tiny pleasures either. Writing it down will take it out of the thought realm and put it into the physical, a big step towards making it a reality. Having a list will help you stay on track to continue to live life to the fullest.

After you've taken action on one of your desires, check it off (orgasmic for you list lovers!) and CELEBRATE. This is crucial! It will create a new association in your mind that it's okay to have fun and explore your passions.

Permitting yourself to step outside your comfort zone is more about the person you will become than what you actually did. One of the best things about embracing life is that it gives you a lift and a feeling of renewal—kind of like a double espresso shot minus the jitters. It's exactly the break your mind needs to become more efficient and less reactive when getting back to the "have-to" stuff. Miraculously all the things you didn't think you would have time to do get done with a lot more ease because your mind is less stressed. This is a total win-win, wonder woman!

Love More

Embracing life is also about living from your heart instead of your head and loving more. It's about expressing the desire to share your exuberance with the world by offering smiles, kindness, and compassion to everyone, from the homeless to your loved ones, without hidden agendas.

There are only two emotions, love and fear—you'll find everything, when rooted out, links back to one of these two feelings. If you want to go for the gusto you'll need to be operating out of love and kick your fears to the curb because that's the only way you'll be able to reclaim your power and live out your heartfelt dreams and desires.

When you are happy and full of pure love you're vibrating at such a high level it can be felt by others without you saying a word. Traveling at lightning speed this magic bullet impacts the universe and every single being in it with its power to heal, overcome fear, and inspire bliss. It's such a juicy force!

When you embrace life, not only are you contributing to the flow of this phenomenal energy, you are expressing who you are in the fullest, most complete way. This alignment allows all things to be possible for you, as though you're in God's jet stream.

Heart Opening Exercise

Give yourself permission to be vulnerable and seen by opening your heart. This creates the connection you crave like nothing else. Sending love to everyone who has ever shown you kindness is a great way to open your heart. Just sit quietly, close your eyes and start remembering everyone who has touched your heart or shown you kindness. Visualize a stream of sparkling pink energy flowing to them. In addition send love to any projects you are working on, your bank accounts, anyone who has wronged you, people you are holding grudges against, and all the people you've not yet met, eventually sending love all around the world. Do this until tears of bliss are flowing down your cheeks. Do this every day for three months and notice how your life expands and changes.

Love Has Four Letters—GIVE

From Gandhi to God it's been said giving is one of the greatest components of love. The more you give, the more your world will become a dazzling place to live. Giving from the heart without any underlying motivation will ignite your diamond power and light you up from the inside out. Sparkling radiance, here you come!

The emphasis is on *not having an agenda*. If you are giving to get, it's likely your results will be disappointing. For example, I had a client who was very generous, helping friends, organizations and colleagues with both her time and money, but would often end up resentful. When I asked her what her motivation was in the giving, she reflected and admitted that when she gave she expected to gain approval, appreciation and love and would get resentful if that outcome didn't happen. However, with this realization came the awareness when she was inspired to give just to give she always felt wonderful.

The irony is that giving from your heart is the best investment you can make. There are no dividends anywhere in the world like it. You will always get back far more than you've given and you will always feel expanded and blissful.

Think how you feel when someone has given you something out of the goodness of his or her heart. Whether it's a gift, an act of kindness, emotional support, or their time, aren't you inspired to give back? It's human nature to mirror so start creating a reflection of giving. Give your gifts and talents freely to loved ones, friends, cohorts, strangers, and the world. Stop hiding your light! Give what you can to others both emotionally and financially and you will start to see those protective walls that keep you small and separate start to crumble. You will feel so good about yourself you will glow with happiness, becoming irresistible.

One of the listeners of my weekly radio program, Mila, sent me an email I will always treasure. This beautiful woman from Sweden had tuned into my Valentine's Day call, which was full of ideas for sparking romance in your relationship.

After listening she decided to write her husband a letter acknowledging everything she appreciated and adored about him (Romance-Capade #3, Love Letter, on page 222). While he was in the shower she snuck in and wrote a passionate message including kisses on the mirror in red lipstick and then framed it with some sexy stickers. She placed her love letter beneath the message and slipped out before he was done. When he got out of the shower he was blown away by her surprise.

When he came out for dinner he was a different man. Normally on the quiet side, he was suddenly Mr. Jovial, talkative and responsive. He opened up to her in ways he never had before. She knew it was all due to the love letter, which had given him the gift of her true admiration of what she really loved and enjoyed about him. By opening up she created a space for him to open. Writing the letter made her feel a bit vulnerable because there is always that little voice saying, "what will he think?" or "will I be rejected?" But she was okay with those reservations, because more than anything she wanted to give him the gift of knowing the love that she felt for him. As for her husband, receiving this gift in the form of a letter gave him the luxury of reading and reveling in her love over and over again. Needless to say, he was overjoyed.

I love this story because in the end, her vulnerability proved to be her strength. How many times have you held back expressing your heartfelt feelings to your loved ones because of a fear that you'll be rejected or it won't be received the way you hoped it would? Yet when you hold back you're actually giving power to your limitations and allowing your head to overrule your heart. You start thinking what the payoff will be for you to express your love; will you get anything in return?

This is what you want to get away from—step out of your

comfort zone and express love without any expectations of what you'll get back. If you are already doing this, fabulous! If not you will be amazed at how good it feels to give with such purity and authenticity. The beauty of this type of giving is that it naturally creates a flow that's going to bring you the love you want in return without you trying to control it. Can you feel the difference? Approaching any relationship, including the relationship you have with yourself, with what you can give rather than what you can get allows the truth to emerge and come forth.

There are a lot of ways to give love—don't make this hard! You can make your man his favorite meal, tell your friend how much you appreciate her friendship, offer your time and services, give your mom a hug for no reason and tell her you love her, provide your sister a shoulder to cry on and be a good listener, hold the elevator, open the door for somebody pregnant or disabled, put money in the meter for a stranger without them knowing, pay the toll for the car behind you—the list is endless. There are a million little ways to show love. These acts of kindness are really just ways of paying it forward. They *will* be repaid at some point—karma is exact— you don't need to figure out when or where or how. You just need to give with no expectation, from a place of willingness and a desire to be a generous spirit.

Gratitude

Outside of love, expressing gratitude is the most beautiful gift you can give yourself and others. Like love, it's a pure, positive, high energy that creates an authentic internal radiance. Have you ever noticed how when you are truly grateful it feels like your heart has cracked wide open and you have the sensation of giving and receiving at the same time? Giving thanks has a ricochet effect; not only does this gorgeous energy bounce back to you, it's now intensified and magnified by your awareness of the magnificence of what you are grateful for.

Spend time every day delighting in being alive and appreciative of all the little things. If you take the time to focus on something you're grateful for, to the point of tears, you will be in the highest vibration, attracting only good. This can happen by looking into the eyes of your child, or playing with your pet, or having a phone chat with your best friend, or sinking into a memory of a moment with your mom or dad where you felt unconditional love, or remembering a kindness from your partner, or standing in nature in awe of what God has created, or...

In this space not only will you feel full, blessed, and peaceful, you will be graced with more and more and more. All sorts of people will show up to help you or give you messages, doors will open, amazing opportunities will come your way. Feeling grateful till your heart opens with joy, on a consistent basis, will bring you all the sparkling realities of your desires much more quickly than merely thinking about them with no feeling. Abundance of love and relationship, health and wealth, success and well-being will all be yours simply because you are grateful and making the choice to experience joy in your life.

If you are in a relationship that feels more like a tug of war than a union of love, you can bring positive movement and life to this dynamic. How? It's easy. Show appreciation and gratitude to your man for his help and efforts.

You may be thinking WHY do you have to thank him for something he should be responsible for as part of the household team—if you're not getting any thanks, why should he? The answer is simple: after interviewing lots of men they've all said the more they are appreciated, the more they want to do. So work it! Tell him he'll be your hero if he takes out the trash, and when he's done thank him. It won't be long before he'll be emptying the trash when it's half full just to hear your praise. Your man will support you when he feels appreciated—in more ways than you could ask for or imagine.

You can show this appreciation to everyone in your life—kids, friends, family, co-workers, boss, store clerks, you name it. The more gratitude and appreciation you express, the more you will get back.

Lots of people suggest journaling your gratitude at night before you go to sleep. While this is a great idea, it's even better to make gratitude a lifestyle. Why not commit to making gratitude a habit that runs throughout your day so you can get the full benefit of this phenomenal energy working for you consistently. Adding the nightly routine will make it even more powerful because whatever you think about five minutes before you drift off at night marinates in your subconscious while you sleep. You definitely want positive thoughts roaming around your dreamscape.

Stepping Outside of Your Comfort Zone

Fully embracing life usually means you have to get outside of your comfort zone. One of the biggest "rut" culprits is routine. Although it provides safety and comfort in knowing what to expect the "typical" delivers little pizazz. Life becomes boring and dull.

All along my journey I've always found when I stepped

outside my comfort zone it was very freeing and I felt so pleased with myself. A few years ago I took a pole-dancing class. At first I was nervous, thinking I was a bit old to be doing this and everyone would probably be gorgeous and young and able to do the routines much better than I. All in my head of course. Yet I mustered my moxie and when I got there I was pleasantly surprised to see most of the women were older housewives. They, just like me, were there to experience a new form of dance to get in touch with their sensuality and feminine power.

At one point as I was spinning around the pole I threw caution to the wind, got some super speed going, and my glasses flew off! I laughed and felt so liberated. To me it was also a message that my physical vision limits me in so many ways—by just going with my inner desire I see so much more clearly and in ways that support and serve my growth.

One of my students, Katrina, was much more comfortable in her masculine than feminine energy. Wanting change badly she courageously stepped outside of her comfort zone by scheduling boudoir photos and signing up to take my teleplayshop, "Discover How to Find and Own Your Playful Sexy Self." During the course she was able to open up in ways that helped her rock her boudoir shoot by connecting with her feminine energy. With this surrender the photos captured her authentic sensual and beautiful essence. After the success of her adventures, Katrina is now on fire—embracing lingerie, creating exciting rendezvous with her significant other, and playfully working her inner sexy. By being brave and stepping outside her comfort zone she is now having the time of her life, feeling alive and whole again.

To embrace life fully, I invite you to a challenge: from now on when you wake up in the morning ask yourself what you can do to get in the mindset of vacation—then do it. Commit to taking one action that will embody your vivacious vacation persona. Before you know it, you'll be living la dolce vita!

Pause and Reflect

1) Close your eyes and remember your favorite vacation. What feelings surface? How can you recreate those same feelings in your daily life?

2) For the next seven days express your gratitude daily to at least three people.

3) Spend five minutes every morning sending love to every person who has been significant in your life. Bonus: send love to those people who have caused you pain or hurt you in some way.

Revel in Your Radiance

Step outside your comfort zone and do something that makes you a little bit nervous. This will propel you forward and gift you with the thrilling sensation that life is coursing through your blood. You have that inner victory screaming "I did it!" giving you confidence, self-esteem and an appreciation for yourself. It also gives you the taste of how juicy life can be when you bite into it, even if it's a nibble at a time.

CHAPTER 11

Sexy and Sparkling Forever

You've come a long way, baby, since you picked up this book! Right now give yourself a standing ovation for the changes you've made working the SPARKLE System. By now you should have a clear vision of your future and an unbridled excitement about life. Your inner "Lois and Clark" (yin and yang) are learning to live in harmony. You're authoring and starring in the most delicious autobiography ever written, and you lead with love, always your language of choice. Now that you've tapped into your buried desires and unleashed your passionate playful Self, renewed your relationship with *you* and truly know who you are, you can live an authentic and celebrated life with confidence and courage. Most importantly, whether single or married you are in control of your life, never to lose yourself again. Revel in your success!

But now that you're dazzling, how will you stay sexy

and sparkling? Like everything after 40 it will take some maintenance! You clean your jewelry of gunk so why wouldn't you do the same for yourself? You've worked hard for your diamond crown. You owe it to yourself to learn how to keep it firmly in place.

If you want to remain radiant all you have to do is make that choice—consistently. The good news is, no matter how much grime gathers on your magnificent Self you've got the SPARKLE System to help you find your way back to your diamond power. This chapter shows you how to maintain your beauty from the inside out, always.

Stay Conscious

Staying conscious means being aware of your thoughts and actions at all times. If the stealth committee invades your mind with thoughts of judgment, criticism and negativity about yourself or others, you have a choice either to listen or form a filibuster against their verbal attack. Why not be proactive? Get clear on your plan of action by asking yourself these questions:

1) What choice will I make when the old voices come calling?
2) What am I committed to?
3) Who am I committed to?
4) Am I honoring my radiance?
5) What choice can I make to stay in integrity with myself?

What I've learned along the way is that life is a process. No matter how much you clean up, there will always be more mud-slinging; it will be up to you to get out the polish and shine yourself up again. It's usually not the same mud—oh no, it has siblings and cousins and third cousins and so many other cousins once removed you wish you were no longer part of the family! But each time you clean one up you're going to create another beautiful cut to your diamond, making you even more valuable. This takes consistent conscious choice, the willingness to change, and the tools to lead you out. You now have those tools with the SPARKLE System.

Work the System!

Whenever you are being challenged simply go back to the SPARKLE System and revisit the section that will help you move forward. It's not necessary to go through every step—the system has been designed so that each section works independently. In a sense it's like going into a diamond mine: dig into the chapter that gives you the magic to turn whatever lump of coal has shown up in your life into a gorgeous gemstone.

For example, if you're depressed and feel you have nothing to look forward to, reread Chapter 4: Seeing Your Bright Future. If you find yourself falling back into old patterns and behaviors, Chapter 7: Renew Your Relationship with YOU will help you break free again. Feeling uptight, rigid, exhausted? A dose of Chapter 9: Laugh and Play will do the trick. If you work the book, your life will work!

What I hope you take away from reading this book is a belief in your own magnificence and an awareness of your extraordinary value. It is my deep desire that you connect with your courage, tap into your creativity, unleash your playfulness, and unearth your deepest desires. That you not only identify your unique song but sing it freely, unabashedly, not afraid to be heard or seen. That you live your life fully Self-expressed as the enchantress you were born to be. Finally, that you embrace your diamond power and know how to keep it shining brilliantly.

Nurture Your Joy

One day when I sat meditating on my patio I heard a loud humming noise. Startled, I opened my eyes expecting to find a big bee buzzing around me. I was delighted to see instead a sweet hummingbird, suspended in air, staring me in the eye. Despite the whirring of her wings there was effortlessness to her suspension. Looking into this lovely creature's eyes I felt such a lift and filled with happiness and joy. As soon as I "got it" she whisked off to her perch in a nearby tree.

Every time I sat outside she came to visit as though it were her mission to remind me that life is to be enjoyed. When I moved I was sad thinking how I would miss my little friend. Believe it or not, the first day I sat outside on my new patio I heard that familiar whirring. I looked up and sure enough, there was a beautiful hummingbird suspended in air. Was it the same hummingbird? I doubt it, but the message was clear. As we leave things behind there is always a new source of joy waiting to greet us ahead.

Ironically, this morning as I was thinking about the ultimate message to give you, a hummingbird suddenly appeared! Of course, joy. Hummingbirds are the symbol of joy. I was so grateful for this instant and perfect answer.

After 40 so many women lose their joy and spark. They start to look outside themselves for ways to bring excitement, happiness and wholeness back into their lives, but that's not where they are going to find lasting joy. True joy starts from within, deeply seeded in your heart. Just as you tend to a garden, if you nurture these seeds with passion, respect and love, they will blossom into an inner haven of happiness. When you have this internal source to draw upon you will never be dependent on anyone or anything to fill you up. You'll make decisions from a place of peace instead of need, helping to ensure you won't regret your choices down the road. Your life will run much more smoothly, with next to no drama.

Staying sparkling means you choose not to engage in:

1) People pleasing—remember, this will cause you to forget who you are. Only do things for others when your heart guides you to do so. Acting out of guilt or obligation ultimately creates resentment because it's offensive to your integrity.
2) Performing for love—get off the hamster wheel and know you are enough!
3) Seeking external validation—don't give someone else the power to determine your value and worth. This can and will crush your soul if you're not careful.
4) Throwing masculine tirades or trying to take a man's power as your own—staying in your feminine is necessary for your relationships to thrive with both women and men. Trust yourself, you don't need to go into the masculine to feel powerful.
5) Separating from others—insisting you can do it all alone is so isolating and disempowering. Reach out and connect!
6) Labeling yourself as your shadow side (or allowing others to label you as such)—you may sabotage yourself by trying to live up to them. If you are going to label yourself, use a nickname that describes who you want to become. How

about something like Vivacious Vixen or Radiant Love or Diamond Duchess?

Loving your Self is the key to radiance. When your abundance comes from within, you will float through life with authentic confidence, happiness and self-worth. This will make you totally irresistible. What's more you'll be living an uncompromising life of integrity.

Now that you've got your sparkle on, you've got the courage and sass to try a sexy adventure. In the following pages you'll find a total of 15 Romance-Capades to get the ball rolling. Have some fun! Let your imagination run wild and add your own twists and turns. You, my sweet, are now sexy and sparkling, living your dazzling diamond power!

Pause and Reflect

1) What is your biggest take-away from this book?

2) Make a plan of action to combat your stealth committee and intercept self-doubt before it buries your sparkle.

3) When at a crossroads choose love. When faced with a challenging situation ask the heavens, "What would love do?" You have the power to change the dynamics of your life and relationship by tapping into love. When in doubt choose LOVE!

Revel in Your Radiance

Leisurely look through the next part of the book, "Passport to Passion." Which Romance-Capades speak to your lust for life? Which themes send a thrill up your spine? Choose one sexy adventure to do with your man. Commit to a date, enlist your sensational soul sister support team, and soar into your sensuality!

THE DIAMOND BELIEF

Repeat these affirmations daily to maintain your sexy, sparkling Self!

Cut:

I now cut away all the limiting beliefs and thoughts that no longer serve me. I am free to be my beautiful, sparkling Self.

Clarity:

I know who I am; I am clear about how to unleash my Diamond Essence to be the sparkling woman I was born to BE.

I live in truth.

Color:

I am the most vibrant Technicolor version of ME—playful, passionate, sexy and sensational. I dazzle with my radiance.

Carat:

I am valuable. I love, honor and respect myself by living in my feminine diamond power. I know I matter and I celebrate my worth. I am a beautiful, sparkling, sexy woman.

The Diamond Belief

I, ___________________________, trust my decisive action, trust the universe to show me "how," trust my dreams will manifest in a way far better than I could ever have engineered for myself. I am one with Source energy, and I see my future strong, loving, filled with romance and passion, travel, family, fun, joy, laughter, creativity, knowing and oneness with my Being. I act now to bring my future to me, I respond by speaking my truth and using my creativity to move forward into the light, into my new life that is filled with love and light. I ask God/Source, my Angels, my Guides and Teachers to help assist me in following my light to my highest and best good that will promote my growth. I see that by using my own inner strengths and taking action now it will promote my growth. I have the ability and I recognize that this is my time to move forward with my life! I see and create an amazing future and build a relationship with my beautiful future Self! I am playful, I am radiant, I am sexy, I am a Sparkling Goddess! Thank you, God!

Download The Diamond Belief @ www.SexyandSparkling.com

Passport to Passion

Romance-Capades™

It All Starts With the Invitation...

The following Romance-Capades offer easy, fun instructions on how to create passionate adventures that will bring fresh sensual sparks to your relationship. You can start off slow, choosing what feels right for you and build from there, or you can throw caution to the wind and jump in with both feet! No matter where you begin, these sexy escapades will send the barometer on your love life soaring!

Chapter 12

The Art of the Invitation

If your relationship already has its bag of tricks to spark your love life, kudos! You're one of the lucky few. But if you and your mate are like the majority of couples, you're experiencing a romantic rut. Let's face it, doing the same things over and over again can become a bit boring. The same old routine can leave you feeling like there's something missing. And truth be told, there *is* something missing—your creative passionate expression!

There are so many different facets to who you are as a sensual being, once you discover and unleash them into your life and relationship you will feel energized, empowered, ultra-feminine and more whole. Either way, Romance-Capades are a juicy addition to your romantic repertoire and a steamy way to whet your amorous appetite.

How to Use the Romance-Capades™

As we saw in Chapter 9: Laugh and Play, there are many ways to flirt. There's the coy cocking of the head, the batting of the eye, the big fresh smile, the direct stare, the sideways glance, the crossing and uncrossing of the legs (*à la* Sharon Stone in *Basic Instinct*), eating with pleasure (Kim Basinger in *9 ½ Weeks*)... and the list goes on. But the most playful and powerful way to flirt engages all the senses: eyes, ears, nose, touch, taste. Thus the Romance-Capade was born!

Years ago I introduced Romance-Capades at romance parties created for women who wanted to spice up their love life and deepen intimacy with their partners. I presented the themed adventures in product form, set up on a table covered with red velvet, rose petals and candles. For example, "Let's Burn It Up" (page 250) included a firefighter's hat filled with a "Light My Fire" CD, a pair of sexy panties, a can of whipped cream dressed up as a fire extinguisher, and other tantalizing goodies. As the women circled the table, I could see both the desire and the doubt on their faces. They loved the romantic ideas but were at a loss as to how to put these teasing trysts into action. Overwhelmingly they requested step-by-step guidance—including tips on what to do with the kids. Once direction was given, they gained confidence and were able to successfully pull off the escapades.

If you too find yourself experiencing feelings of insecurity at first, know you are in good company. I know it can be a little scary—heck, my friends and I have been known to down a little liquid courage before our Romance-Capades! But here's the deal—your guy loves YOU. He's not looking at what you consider to be imperfections, and he's not judging you. He's admiring and appreciating your adventurous and playful spirit. He's feeling warm and wonderful that you've taken the time to plan this intriguing interlude for him. And he's feeling hot and bothered knowing that there's a big time "win" for him at the end of this sexy story. Believe me, he's all over it. You have just been placed on the goddess pedestal. Guaranteed.

All you have to do is breathe, follow the steps, open to your womanhood, and let your imagination run wild. Once you've jumped in, you'll be thrilled to see how much fun you have creating your feminine lair. Those days of waiting for your man to turn into Don Juan are over! Take charge of your heat and you will feel enlivened, vibrant and empowered.

You may want to read through all of the Romance-Capades before making your choice. As you flip through the following saucy scenarios, start off with one that feels comfortable but stretches you a wee bit. Ideally it will stir your imagination and fire your senses. If you are not used to engaging your playful side, choose one of the milder themes—or dare to be bold with one of the more outrageous ones. Remember, you are a leading lady. Access your attitude!

Romantic Adventure 101

Let's explore the elements of a Romance-Capade. You can follow the instructions to the letter or use your imagination to add your own twists and turns. The goal is to get your sensual Self in action!

It all starts with the *Passport to Passion* invitation. This is no ordinary invite, but a come-hither that promises mystery and intrigue, adventure and excitement, sass and sexiness. Similar to an exotic travel destination photo that triggers wanderlust, the Passport to Passion invitation sparks a sense of desire and urgency, prompting the invitee to exclaim, "Get me there quick!" When you send it off the magic begins...it will pique your honey's interest and let him know you are planning something special just for him.

The invitation is perfect for any celebration, be it a birthday, anniversary, career promotion, holiday, honeymoon, or just because...especially just because. A well-crafted invitation will set the mood for your man and turn his ordinary day into one of extraordinary excitement. Not only will it send his testosterone soaring, it will make him feel special and appreciated. Giving your partner a heads up will also help the evening go more smoothly. There's less chance of him working late, bringing a friend home, or showing up cranky when he knows you're cookin' up something hot that will take the sizzle from the kitchen to the bedroom!

Each Romance-Capade includes a fun, flirty invitation and suggestions on how to deliver it. You can download all of the invitations and sizzling recipes for free at www.SexyandSparkling.com, or you can unleash your imagination and create your own.

The number of flame icons tells you how "hot" each adventure is. One flame indicates a warm, romantic evening to ease you and your honey into togetherness. Two flames promises a steamy adventure involving a bit more imagination and vavoom. Three flames means you are *smokin'*, girl! It's a three-alarm fire sure to set your man aflame.

The *title* of each Romance-Capade and the brief *synopsis* below it clue you into the theme of each adventure. Paris at Dawn, Meet Me at the Kasbah, Island Fever...you can see it, taste it, feel it, yes?

Here are the other elements of each Romance-Capade, in order:

- The *"Recipe for Romance" Essentials* are the ingredient goodies to help you build your sensual bonfire. Each theme has its own unique list.
- *Mix It Up* gives you creative ideas on how to make your adventure fun and sexy.
- *Passport to Passion Invitation* includes an arrival stamp where you can put the date of your escapade creating intrigue and excitement for the sexy soirée you've planned.
- *Set the Mood for Romance* guides you on choosing just the right lighting, location, music and other props.
- *Get Your Sparkle On!* describes the perfect outfit, persona, and attitude to don to take your man's breath away.
- *Feed His Passion* offers celebrity chef suggestions for delicious themed drinks and nibbles sure to whet his appetite…for you! Recipes found at www.SexyandSparkling.com.
- *How to Prepare for Your Romantic Adventure* gives you a handy timeline two weeks out to the day of the big event.
- If your nerves get the best of you, *Cold Feet* will guide you right through them.
- *You Can Do It!* offers tips on ways to pull off your saucy escapade with style.
- *Celebrate* reminds you to honor your brave, bold spirit for taking action, no matter what.
- Keep the love burning and the momentum going with *What's Next?*
- Your password is…romance. You'll need to use this password to access the *Passport to Passion Invitations* found at www.SexyandSparkling.com.

There you have it—the 101 on Romance-Capades. It's up to you and your lush imagination to bring it to life. The Romance-Capade is a perfect way to rev up your romantic life, however it plays out. If there are twists and turns, you'll be much more relaxed if you have a backup plan. Many of my clients revealed when things didn't go exactly as expected they moved into Plan B. Remember, attitude is everything and the key to the success of your interlude is staying positive and playful. By having some options you'll be able to remain fluid and flowing, keeping your focus on the end result—fun romantic adventure. Embrace your feminine power at all times!

Just follow the steps, keeping your mind and heart open to inspiration, making it more your own. Get ready for some sizzling, sensual connection!

Romance-Capade #1:

Bring Back the Spark!

Rekindle your relationship by designing a romantic evening reminiscent of those heady days of dating. Fan the embers by mixing things up, playfully rediscovering each other and remembering why you fell in love in the first place...

"Recipe for Romance" Essentials

Follow this recipe to the T or whip up your own creation by adding or substituting goodies.

candlelight
rose petals
music

Mix It Up

Simply dining in another room of your home is a great way to rev up your relationship. If you're like most couples you've gotten into a romantic rut with routine. Eating dinner in the same spot day after day, with no meaningful conversation, tuning into the TV instead of each other—doesn't exactly bring on the "tingles," does it? To rekindle the warmth and closeness you once knew together, you're going to have to mix things up. If this makes you nervous enlist a friend for support. Your decision to stoke the embers may inspire her to do the same. Repeat this Romance-Capade often to keep the sparks flying.

Passport to Passion Invitation

Pique his curiosity by delivering your invitation in one of these ways:

- Put it in his pocket as he's leaving the house.
- Prop it against the coffee maker with a red rose.
- Let your imagination run wild!

How to Set the Mood for Romance

- Lighting: candlelight
- Music: songs that inspire happy memories
- Location: any room other than where you currently eat dinner—weather permitting, dining on the patio can be very romantic.
- Tease: flower petals scattered on the table and floor

Get Your Sparkle On!

- Wardrobe ideas: soft, feminine flowing dress with pretty shoe, preferably high heels
- Persona: "I'm excited to see you."
- Attitude: fun, flirty and adoring

Feed His Passion...and Yours

You can find delicious, celebrity chef beverage and dish recipes at www.SexyandSparkling.com.

- Beverage: your favorite drinks
- Dinner: his favorite meal

How to Prepare for Your Romantic Adventure

Two weeks in advance:

- Order/shop or search your closet for your ensemble.
- If you're a mom, schedule a babysitter for the night of your adventure or, better yet, arrange for your kids to stay with family or friends.

One week in advance:

- Design dinner plan and choose your new dining location.
- Get your props together (candles and rose petals).

Day before:

- Prepare invitation.
- Prepare outfit.
- Shop for food.

Day of Romance-Capade:

- Deliver invitation.
- Set table and create ambiance.
- Prepare dinner.

Cold Feet?

Nervous? That's perfectly normal! Take a deep breath and remind yourself why you wanted to create this romantic evening in the first place. Not only will your courage rev up your relationship and provide an opening for reconnection, it will build your confidence and make you feel vibrant and alive. That said, having a support system in place will help calm those jitters. Here are a few suggestions:

- Ask one of your girlfriends to be on standby for a last-minute phone call or text message.
- Give yourself a heartfelt pep talk.
- Exercise.
- Reminisce by going through photo albums and remembering all the happy times.
- Do a meditation/visualization just before he arrives.

You Can Do It!

Give yourself permission to see and feel the outcome you want, leaving your troubles checked at the door. With this vision in mind, create newness and excitement by setting a cozy table in front of the fireplace, in your bedroom, on the patio, or anywhere different from the norm. Be silly and lighthearted. Play music from your dating days, a favorite concert or your wedding song…dance flirtatiously. Make a pact before you sit down that the kids, in-laws and career are taboo topics. With genuine interest, get to know each other again. Rediscover the magic!

* * *

Celebrate

Congratulations! Whatever the outcome of your romantic evening, take the time to honor yourself for taking action. That might mean letting out a whopping wooohooo, jumping in the air, calling and sharing your adventure with a friend, treating yourself to a bouquet of flowers, sending yourself a special congratulatory card—it doesn't matter what you do, just do *something* to celebrate YOU. Journal your experience—how it made you feel, what worked well, and what you might do differently next time. But most of all, love on yourself for bringing sparkle back to your life and your relationship.

What's Next?

Now that you've gotten your confidence back make sure to plan your next Romance-Capade. Get out your calendar, choose a date, and circle it. Do it now! If you wait, months will fly by in a heartbeat without an encore. After rekindling your love life do you really want to let it cool again? To ensure your life and relationship stay passionately alive you'll need consistent planning. Think about it, if you want a gorgeous garden you need to spend time nurturing it, right? Your relationship is no different. So flip through the following pages, choose another delicious adventure, and watch your love life blossom!

ROMANCE-CAPADE #2:

Dream Angel

Surprise your guy by slipping on some luscious new lingerie and lounge flirtatiously. Drive him wild with some seductive poses and sneak peeks, setting the tone for a steamy night!

"Recipe for Romance" Essentials

Follow this recipe to the T or whip up your own creation by adding or substituting goodies.

candles
music
lingerie

Mix It Up

Since men are visual the simplest way to create a stir in your love life is to slip into some lacy lingerie. It doesn't require much time or thought yet will infuse your relationship with the passion that may be missing. Trust me, he will *love* it! Recruit a friend who may encourage you to be a *bit* bolder and start shopping for something frisky. Black is the sexiest color but if you feel like a walk on the wild side, go for red or an animal print. This juicy surprise will thrill your man either at home or on a romantic weekend getaway.

Passport to Passion Invitation

Pique his curiosity with these delivery options:

- Attach the invitation to a pretty pair of panties and hang it from his rear view mirror.
- Wrap a scented silky stocking in a bow around the invite and send to his office.
- Let your imagination run wild!

How to Set the Mood for Romance

- Lighting: candlelight, switch out white light bulbs with sultry red ones

- Music: Gato Barbieri's "Europa" (very sexy saxophone), Marvin Gaye, download romantic mood music from iTunes
- Location: bedroom or hotel getaway
- Tease: send text with picture of lingerie or dangle well-known lingerie store bag (*à la* Victoria's Secret) in front of him saying, "I have a surprise for you tonight!"

Get Your Sparkle On!

- Wardrobe ideas: pretty black push-up bra, lacy undies, thigh-high stockings and high, high heels; short nighty with built-in bra cup; teddy with garter belt. If more adventurous choose an animal print. Accessorize with delicate anklet.
- Persona: Dream Angel
- Attitude: alluring and flirty

Feed His Passion...and Yours

Create intimacy and excitement by sensually feeding each other these nibbles. (Recipes found at www.SexyandSparkling.com.)

- Beverage: Elderflower Champagne Cocktail or non-alcoholic sparkling wine

- Appetizer: chocolate dipped strawberries, candied ginger, cashews, Mimolette & grapes

How to Prepare for Your Romantic Adventure

Two weeks in advance:

- Order/shop for new lingerie.
- If you're a mom, schedule a babysitter for the night of your adventure or, better yet, arrange for your kids to stay with family or friends.

One week in advance:

- Get your props together (candles and red light bulbs).

Day before:

- Prepare invitation.
- Prepare outfit.
- Shop for food.

Day of Romance-Capade:

- Deliver invitation.
- Practice your hot flirt.
- Set up lighting.
- Prepare appetizers.

Cold Feet?

Wanna chicken out? Everyone does! Remember the stealth committee—those nasty little demons in your mind that want to "protect" you? Befriend them, reassure them and let them know they need to get current with the new you... the you that's ready to unleash her fabulous femininity and sexy, sparkling Self. Kick your fears and doubts to the curb with a fantastic support system. Here are a few helpful suggestions:

- Ask a soul sister you can depend on to be available for a pep talk.
- Take a deep breath and exhale a loud, sensual "Haaaa."
- Body movements/dance to connect you with your sensuality.
- Do yoga or other centering exercise.
- Do a meditation/visualization just before he arrives.

You Can Do It!

Celebrate your curves in anything from a push-up bra to a naughty negligee, then cover up with a silky robe and let yourself feel empowered by your big sexy secret. At bedtime lounge flirtatiously and tease with a few sneak peeks to drive him wild, help you reconnect to your sensuality and get the night rolling. Trust your instincts and have fun. If you're feeling frisky, increase the heat by creating a catwalk and strutting like a Victoria's Secret model. Sexiness is all about doing what you want and enjoying yourself so let that sultry side out. Get ready for your pedestal, goddess!

Celebrate

Wooohooo, you did it! Congratulations! Whether things went exactly as planned or you had to move to Plan B, do something to CELEBRATE. Stretching yourself through this experience added another beautiful facet to your diamond power. Why not buy yourself something sparkling to honor and remind you of your action? A small diamond paperweight, phone case, cz's or the real thing! Even a shimmering note card placed on your nightstand will bring daily celebration to your heart.

What's Next?

Take the time now, while you're feeling sassy and empowered, to flip through the following pages and choose your next Romance-Capade. What buried gem wants to be dusted off and given a chance to shine next time? Get excited—you're not only liberating all the different facets of your personality, you're bringing romance, passion and dimension to your relationship. Get your calendar or planner out, pick a date and circle it with a big red heart!

Love Letter

Capture your lover's heart with sentiments from your soul... make him feel like your hero by expressing your adoration in a good old-fashioned handwritten love letter. This beautiful gift will come back to you tenfold with a magical night of romance and passion.

"Recipe for Romance" Essentials

Follow this recipe to the T or whip up your own creation by adding or substituting goodies.

1 sheet Old World stationery
¼″ wide strand of burgundy ribbon
1 gold heart charm
1 love letter box
1 package red silk rose petals

Mix It Up

Nothing says romance like a love letter. Go to a bookstore and pore over the greatest love letters ever written for inspiration. Reflect on your relationship and pen a letter on Old World stationery, sharing your heartfelt feelings. Let him know how much he means to you, how much you appreciate him, and how grateful you are to have him in your life. Roll it up and tie it off with ribbon and a gold heart charm, lay it on a bed of red silk roses in a decorative box and send it with a kiss. (Items can be found at a craft store.)

Passport to Passion Invitation

Delivery options for this romantic invite:

- Put it in his briefcase.
- Prop it against the coffee maker with a red rose.
- Let your imagination run wild.

How to Set the Mood for Romance

- Lighting: lots of candlelight and votives
- Music: Norah Jones' "Come Away with Me," Beyoncé's "Crazy in Love," Katy Perry's "Teenage Dream"
- Location: dining room/living room/bedroom
- Tease: lipstick a sexy message on mirror

Get Your Sparkle On!

- Wardrobe ideas: soft and pretty, anything with lace or sheer fabric, curled hair
- Persona: feminine
- Attitude: charming, demure, coquettish

Feed His Passion...and Yours

These suggested sensual delectables will fan the flames of his love for you. (Recipes found at www.SexyandSparkling.com.)

- Beverage: Chianti or non alcoholic Almost Sicilian Splash
- Appetizers: Baby Bellas—artichoke and sun-dried tomato stuffed Crimini mushrooms
- Dinner: Arugala Ensalata with Proscuitto, Fig, Fennel and Goat

Cheese, Ricotta Pasta Pillows with Porcini Browned Butter Sauce, Drunken Dark Chocolate n' Mascarpane Mousse with Brandied Bing Cherry

How to Prepare for Your Romantic Adventure

Two weeks in advance:

- Order/shop or search your closet for your ensemble.
- If you're a mom, schedule a babysitter for the night of your adventure or, better yet, arrange for your kids to stay with family or friends.

One week in advance:

- Get your props and romance essentials together.

Day before:

- Prepare invitation.
- Prepare outfit.
- Shop for food.

Day of Romance-Capade:

- Deliver invitation.
- Prepare appetizers.
- Set up props.

Cold Feet?

Butterflies in your stomach? It's normal to feel a bit nervous when you step outside your comfort zone. Breathe! Letting your guy know how much you love and appreciate him will shift the dynamics of your relationship for the better. So close your eyes and jump! Romance and passion await, as well as a big personal bonus for your bravery—increased confidence. Make sure you have a support system in place to help you calm your nerves. Here are a few tips:

- Ask one of your girlfriends to be on standby for a pep talk.
- Give yourself some positive self-talk.
- Make a list of all the benefits this adventure will bring to you and your relationship.
- Do yoga or other centering exercise.
- Do a meditation/visualization just before he arrives.

You Can Do It!

Focus on romance! Leave your love letter where he'll easily see it when he arrives home. When he comes to find you surprise him with a romantic dinner reminiscent of Italy. If you have a fireplace, set the table in front of a roaring fire or do something out of the box and dine in your boudoir. Increase intimacy by touching throughout dinner—playing footsies, touching knees and holding hands. Speak from your heart and continue to make him feel like the man of your dreams with sincere gushing. Love is going to boomerang back to you big time!

* * *

Celebrate

Way to go, *bella*, you did it! Congratulations! Taking action on your desires deserves honoring and CELEBRATION, regardless how the evening turned out. You stretched beautifully and need to acknowledge yourself for bringing romance, passion and LIFE to your relationship. Take time to share your story over a glass of sparkling Prosecco with your girlfriends or buy yourself an Italian charm or heart pendant to remind you of your vibrant spirit. Ahhh….*la dolce vita!*

What's Next?

After bringing such beautiful romance and intimacy to your relationship, you'll want to keep the passion alive. Take the time now, while you're feeling confident and courageous, to choose your next Romance-Capade. Don't wait! With your busy life months will fly by in the blink of an eye so flip through the following pages and choose another delicious adventure that will knock your man's socks off.

Neptune's Desire

🔥🔥

Turn yourself into a shimmering mermaid and lounge playfully on the edge of a sensual bath. Lure your love to your enchanted waters with a trail of shells and pearls. When he arrives greet him with a fun and flirty splash, setting the mood for an evening of romance and passion. Let the tail fights begin!

"Recipe for Romance" Essentials

Follow this recipe to the T or whip up your own creation by adding or substituting goodies.

1 tiara
1 jeweled belly button adornment
1 sexy sea-wear costume/ensemble
1 bottle shimmering body glitter
1 bag shells and pearls
Airbrush Body Tanner
2 bottles of bubbles with wands
3-5 heart-shaped floating candles
3 drops Sensation essential oil in the bath as fragrant aphrodisiac (http://unleashyourselfoils.younglivingworld.com)

Mix It Up

Feel the excitement build as you gather your goodies! Take a friend to help you pick out the perfect color of shimmering body glitter (try a bath & body shop or Walmart). Decide on your sexy sea-wear. If you're wrapping yourself in a toga visit a fabric house for some glitzy cloth or check out an online costume shop—they have lots of fabulous mermaid ensembles. Whatever you do, don't forget your tiara!

Passport to Passion Invitation

Entice your man to this wet and wild escapade in one of the following ways:

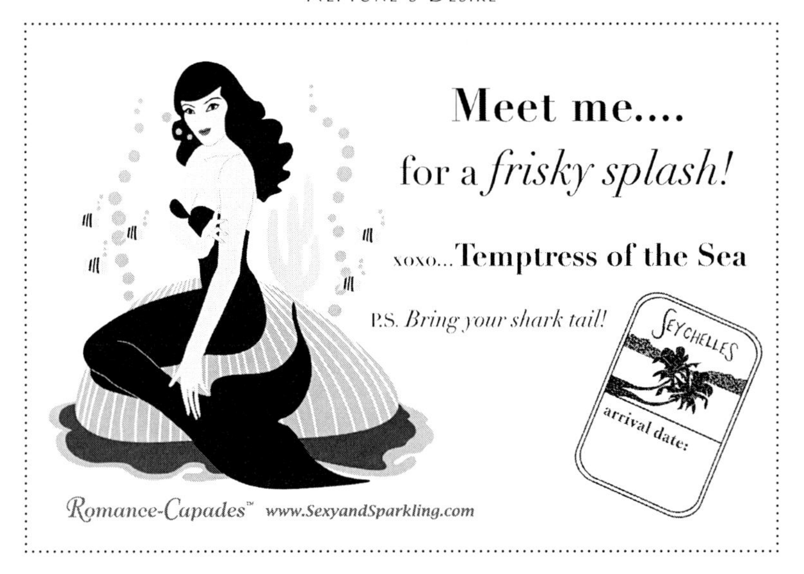

• Put the invite in a clamshell and send it special delivery to his office.

• Wrap it in green or blue tissue paper with pearlized ribbon and put it in his briefcase or on his windshield.

• Let your imagination run wild.

How to Set the Mood for Romance

• Lighting: candlelight sets the mood with floating heart candles in tub

• Music: Robert Plant's "Sea of Love" or go to iTunes and download sea-worthy songs on your iPod

• Location: bathroom or Jacuzzi

• Tease: trail of shells and loose pearls

Get Your Sparkle On!

• Wardrobe ideas: long blonde wig, sexy mermaid costume, bathing suit, or make a toga by wrapping yourself in some sheer fabric. If you're really feeling sassy adorn yourself with a seaweed boa...and nothing else (Google to buy online). Spray gold glitter in the wig for extra sparkle. Go barefoot but make sure toes are pretty and pedicured! Use a sea color polish—think greens and blues.

- Persona: Temptress of the Sea
- Attitude: seductive and mystifying

Feed His Passion…and Yours

Creatively feed each other the suggested ocean treats and savor every bite…this will set an intimate tone for the interlude. (Recipes found at www.SexyandSparkling.com.)

- Beverage: Sex on the Beach—if alcohol is not your thing, try Safe Sex on the Beach
- Appetizers: Shrimp Ceviche Cocktail with Mango-Serrano Salsino, Oysters, Prosciutto, Bathtub Fruit Kabobs

How to Prepare for Your Romantic Adventure

Two weeks in advance:

- Order/shop or search your closet for your ensemble.
- If you're a mom, schedule a babysitter for the night of your adventure or, better yet, arrange for your kids to stay with family or friends.

One week in advance:

- Get your props and romance essentials together.

Day before:

- Prepare invitation.
- Prepare outfit.
- Shop for food.

Day of Romance-Capade:

- Deliver invitation.
- Prepare appetizers.
- Set up props and create trail of shells.

Cold Feet?

Have a support system in place in case you start having second thoughts or feel a bit nervous. Any time you stretch your comfort zone you're going to get anxious—that's normal. Trust that your personal and relationship growth is well worth any jitters. Here are a few suggestions to help you calm your nerves before stepping into your romantic interlude:

- Ask one of your girlfriends to be on standby for support.
- Replace nervous Nellie chatter with positive self-talk.
- Exercise!
- See yourself smiling and happy at the end of the night.
- Breathe in deeply and exhale a loud, sensual "Haaaa"

You Can Do It!

Visualize the outcome you desire. Imagine the look on your lover's face as he finds you glistening in the soft light of the floating heart candles. Just like a mysterious mermaid, imagine you've emerged from the great ocean floor, to tempt, tease and charm. Have some fun blowing bubbles and frolicking in your water playground, before your tails take off to tango!

* * *

Celebrate

Whether your Romance-Capade was a hit or had some twists and turns, celebrate, temptress! You were bold and daring and had the courage to step outside your comfort zone to express your feminine playful spirit and bring a fresh new experience to your relationship. You are AMAZING! Treat yourself to lunch with a friend, a long walk in nature, a decadent dessert, a massage, a bouquet of your favorite flowers. It doesn't matter what you do, it only matters that you do *something* to celebrate YOU.

What's Next?

Now that you've got your mojo flowing, get out your planner, set a date for your next Romance-Capade and keep the momentum going. Life can get really busy and without a commitment you might be tempted to let "stuff" get in the way. To have the passionate love-filled life you desire, choose another romantic adventure and design your relationship destiny.

Island Fever

🔥🔥

Bring the balmy, romantic nights of Hawaii to your home by designing a luau complete with aloha festive drinks, tasty appetizers and relaxing native tunes. Ignite his passion with a sexy hula show, setting the stage for a night of hot island fever!

"Recipe for Romance" Essentials

Follow this recipe to the T or whip up your own creation by adding or substituting goodies.

1 island girl ensemble
2 flower leis
tiki torches
island inspired candles
Hawaiian music

Mix It Up

Make this a fun adventure by getting a girlfriend or two to take hula classes with you OR gather at one of your homes and tune into a YouTube video to learn this sensual island dance. They may have a special someone they want to surprise too so you can practice your moves together. Equally great to do it on your own—either way take some time to watch yourself in a mirror and see what variations are the most flirtatious and fun for you. Pretty hand movements will mesmerize his attention.

Passport to Passion Invitation

Pique his curiosity with these delivery options:

- Prop invite in the bathroom with an orchid for a morning surprise.
- Attach invite to silk lei and put in his briefcase or gym bag.
- Let your imagination run wild!

How to Set the Mood for Romance

- Lighting: tiki torches, island inspired candles
- Music: online Hawaiian music station
- Location: outdoors/backyard if weather permits or turn your living room into a tropical paradise
- Tease: hula dance

Get Your Sparkle On!

- Wardrobe ideas: sarong, bikini or tankini top. If feeling adventurous order a grass skirt and coconut shell bra online. Go barefoot with bright colored pedi: red, orange or coral. Make sure your hands are prettily polished as well. You'll need a lei for you and your love—you can either buy one at your local florist or go to a craft store and get them in silk. If you really want to go all out adorn yourself with a wrist or ankle lei and get a Haiku, hibiscus or orchid for your hair.
- Persona—fully feminine, soft and sensual
- Attitude—friendly, pleasing, relaxed

Feed His Passion…and Yours

Tease as you feed each other, creating a playful and passionate tone. (Recipes found at www.SexyandSparkling.com.)

- Beverage: Blue Hawaiian or non-alcoholic Hibiscus Cooler. Make your drinks festive by adding a paper parasol and garnishing with a pineapple and cherry fruit spear.
- Appetizers: Macadamia Nut-encrusted Mahi-Mahi with Coconut Risotto, Hawaiian Chicken, Coconut Pudding

How to Prepare for Your Romantic Adventure

Two weeks in advance:

- Order/shop or search your closet for your ensemble.
- If you're a mom, schedule a babysitter for the night of your adventure or, better yet, arrange for your kids to stay with family or friends.

One week in advance:

- Get your props and romance essentials together.

Day before:

- Prepare invitation.
- Prepare outfit.
- Shop for food.

Day of Romance-Capade:

- Deliver invitation.
- Prepare appetizers.
- Set up props.

Cold Feet?

Second thoughts? Whenever we let out a new side of ourselves it's normal to get a little nervous. Relax into your island adventure by following these helpful suggestions:

- Ask a soul sister to be on standby to give you a pep talk.
- Take a deep breath and exhale a loud, sensual "Haaaa."
- Sway slowly to a soft Hawaiian tune.
- Do yoga or other centering exercise.
- Do a meditation/visualization just before he arrives.

You Can Do It!

Imagine you and your honey having the time of your life on the islands. Let your vision fill you with excitement. Carry that feeling into the escapade as you greet him with a flower lei and a big "Aloha" kiss. Kindly ask him to leave his shoes at the door and lead him to your tropical paradise. Let the night unfold with pleasure as you wow your handsome hunk with a hip-swaying hula dance and delicious massage. Soft, feminine flirting, albeit shameless, will bring your strong man to his knees, begging for more!

* * *

Celebrate

Wooohooo! Whatever the outcome of your tropical tryst, take a moment to honor yourself for your moxie. Give yourself a hug, jump in the air, dance to your favorite song, call and share your adventure with a friend, buy yourself a gorgeous orchid, send yourself a special card—do a little something just to celebrate YOU.

What's Next?

Now that you've boosted your confidence plan your next Romance-Capade. Do it now! After adding dazzle to your love life do you really want to let it dim again? See what buried beauty wants to debut next! Keep your relationship sexy and sparkling by choosing another delicious adventure and designing your love life on purpose!

Casino Royale

This adventure is designed for those with little time. Lighting, lipstick and naughty glow-in-the-dark dice are all you need to create a risqué rendezvous in your boudoir enticing the likes of "007." Up the ante with a manly cocktail, and together you and your Bondman will have a winning night to remember.

"Recipe for Romance" Essentials

Follow this recipe to the T or whip up your own creation by adding or substituting goodies.

1 pair glow-in-the-dark naughty dice
1 candle of love
1 red lipstick
1 gambling song
1 pair of martini glasses
1 tray
lingerie
stilettos
deck of cards

Mix It Up

This is going to be a saucy, exciting adventure from planning to playing! Start by renting James Bond movies and decide which Bond bombshell you want to be—Vesper Lynd, Pussy Galore, Holly Goodhead, Honey Ryder… then get her persona down. Of course you'll be adding your own unique personality but the movie will give you some direction. Get your naughty dice online. The other romantic essentials can easily be found at local stores. Invite a girlfriend to help you shop for the perfect luscious lingerie. She can hold your hand as you decide on something that might be outside your comfort zone. What fun the "debrief" will be!

Passport to Passion Invitation

Pique his curiosity with these delivery options:

- Spray paint a toy gun gold. Roll the invitation and put it in the nose of the gun. Deliver it to his office or leave it on the seat of his car.
- Roll up the invitation and put it in a martini shaker. Place in refrigerator with a note that says "open me."
- Place in a manila envelope marked "007" and place in his briefcase or on his windshield.

How to Set the Mood for Romance

- Lighting: 25-watt light bulbs and/or red light bulbs and a red candle of love
- Music: "Luck be a Lady" (Frank Sinatra), "Gambler" (Madonna), *Casino Royale* soundtrack
- Location: boudoir
- Tease: Queen of Hearts card in bra

Get Your Sparkle On!

- Wardrobe ideas: pretty bra and panty set with garter belt, thigh-highs and high heels. Silky robe. Take a deck of playing cards and strategically place a few Aces in your lingerie.

- Persona: Bond Girl—choose your favorite
- Attitude: spirited, mysterious, fun, sensual

Feed His Passion…and Yours

Flirt as you feed each other the suggested nibbles below, creating a torrid tone for the night. (Recipes found at www.SexyandSparkling.com.)

- Beverage: Vesper Martini of course! (It's vodka and gin with a twist of a lemon rather than an olive.) If alcohol is not your thing mix up a Cranberry Kiss cocktail.
- Appetizers: caviar, paté, mixed nuts, olives

How to Prepare for Your Romantic Adventure

Two weeks in advance:

- Order/shop or search your closet for your ensemble.
- If you're a mom, schedule a babysitter for the night of your adventure or, better yet, arrange for your kids to stay with family or friends.

One week in advance:

- Get your props and romance essentials together.

Day before:

- Prepare invitation.
- Prepare outfit.
- Shop for food.

Day of Romance-Capade:

- Deliver invitation.
- Prepare appetizers.
- Set up props.

Cold Feet?

Got the jitters? It's just the stealth committee in your mind trying to "protect" you. You can handle them—you're a Bond girl! Kick your fears to the curb with a fantastic support system. Here are a few suggestions:

- Ask one of your cheerleading girlfriends to be on standby for support.
- Breathe in deeply and exhale a loud, sensual "Haaaa."
- Dance to your favorite Bond music.
- Do yoga or other centering exercise.
- Do a meditation or visualization just before he arrives.

You Can Do It!

Before your man retires for the night, sneak into the bathroom and scrawl an invitation in red lipstick across the mirror such as "007, Your mission awaits...meet me between the sheets for details!" Before he bolts out of the bathroom in excited anticipation, place the naughty dice in a martini glass on a tray in the center of your bed, dim the lights, ignite your candle of love, and lie waiting in a provocative pose with a few key playing cards peeking out. Let those dice fly!

* * *

Celebrate

Mission accomplished! Take time to enjoy the spoils of your daring and courageous spirit. Acknowledge and honor the action you took to bring romantic adventure to your relationship. Celebrate by having lunch with your posse of girlfriends and brag on yourself—you may just inspire them to explore their buried passions. Buy yourself a pretty pair of earrings or those cute shoes you've been admiring or a gorgeous rosebud you can watch blossom as you just have. Celebrate YOU!

What's Next?

Now that you've stepped into your stilettos keep them on! Give all your sexy personas a chance to shine by immediately picking another Romance-Capade. Get to know all of you and you'll be thrilled to see how your creative expression brings back your radiance and joy AND keeps your relationship revved up and thriving. Pick a date! Mark your calendar! Start planning!

It Takes Two to Tango

Invite your sexy mate to join you in "The Dance of Love." Set the mood with erotic tango tunes and soft candlelight. Tantalize him with thigh-high fishnets, sexy black lace gloves, a flirtatious fan and a long stem rose clenched between your teeth. Cheek-to-cheek, let your dance of passion begin…

"Recipe for Romance" Essentials

Follow this recipe to the T or whip up your own creation by adding or substituting goodies.

1 pair black lace fingerless gloves (elbow length)
1 pair thigh-high fishnets
1 lace flirty fan
1 red rose (preferably silk, if fresh make sure to de-thorn!)
1 tantalizing tango ensemble
tango music
3-5 candles

Mix It Up

The tango is all about attitude, drama, sensuality and passion. If you're not familiar with it go to YouTube.com and watch the dancing masters for tips. You may want to practice some dramatic expressions and sensual moves beforehand so you're comfortable with your vavoom. The clips will also give you ideas for your outfit. Most of the romance essential items can be found online at Amazon.com or costume stores.

Passport to Passion Invitation

Pique his curiosity with these delivery options:

- Make a perfumed lace envelope, enclose invite and leave it on his car seat with a red rose.
- Kiss the invite with red lipstick and put it in his briefcase or gym bag or jacket pocket.

- Let your imagination run wild.

How to Set the Mood for Romance

- Lighting: dim the lights and place candles around the room
- Music: download a compilation of tango music from iTunes or go to Amazon.com—they have lots to choose from
- Location: living room
- Tease: flirty fan

Get Your Sparkle On!

- Wardrobe ideas: Slick back your hair in a tight bun or get a black wig. Wear a red or black cocktail dress with a flirty skirt so you can easily move your legs. Thigh-high fishnets and a sexy shoe you are comfortable dancing in, black lace fingerless gloves and red nails, and red rose in hair complete the smoldering ensemble.
- Persona: dramatic
- Attitude: sensual and elegant

Feed His Passion...and Yours

Create intimacy and excitement by sensually sharing these bite-size appetizers. (Recipes found at www.SexyandSparkling.com.)

- Beverage: Sangria—or non-alcoholic sparkling wine
- Appetizers: "Exotic Pleasure Wrap," "Love me Tender" peppered filet mignon canapé with horseradish crème, mini raviolis, fig with blue cheese and candied almonds.

How to Prepare for Your Romantic Adventure

Two weeks in advance:

- Order/shop or search your closet for your ensemble.
- If you're a mom, schedule a babysitter for the night of your adventure or, better yet, arrange for your kids to stay with family or friends.

One week in advance:

- Get your props and romance essentials together.

Day before:

- Prepare invitation.
- Prepare outfit.
- Shop for food.

Day of Romance-Capade:

- Deliver invitation.
- Prepare appetizers.
- Set up props.

Cold Feet?

Having second thoughts? Any time you step outside your comfort zone it's normal to feel nervous. Take a few deep breaths and remind yourself of the end result you desire. You can do this! Have faith and take a leap! To bolster your bravery have a backup system in place:

- Ask a supportive friend to be on standby for a pep talk or an encouraging text.
- Say the word "yes" repeatedly for inner strength.
- Watch the movie *True Lies* for inspiration—wonderful tango scenes.

- Breathe in deeply and let out a loud, pleasured "Haaaaa."
- Do a meditation/visualization just before he arrives.

You Can Do It!

Hold on to your fishnets! This is going to be a night to remember. Introduce the sensual and dramatic flavor of the tango by welcoming your Latin lover at the door with a rose between your teeth and a smoldering gaze. Let the pulse of the music create the feeling of the evening. As you dance, flirt with some lusty leg wraps while your face and body tell a story of power and passion. Feel the heat!

* * *

Celebrate

You did it! Whether things went exactly as planned or you had to move into Plan B, do something to CELEBRATE. Stretching yourself through this experience added another beautiful facet to your diamond power. Why not buy yourself something sparkling to honor and remind you of your action? A small diamond paperweight, phone case, cz's or the real thing! A single rose in a vase on your nightstand will remind you to rejoice in YOU!

What's Next?

Right now, while you're feeling fully alive and vibrant, flip through the pages and choose your next Romance-Capade. To ensure your life and relationship stay passionately alive you'll need to nurture it consistently. Think about it, if you want a healthy garden you need to spend time tending it, right? Your relationship is no different. So look ahead, select another spicy adventure, and watch your love grow!

Let's Get Twisted

🔥🔥

Invite your lover to play an age-old game with new racy rules. Set the mood with lively Latin tunes, dancing flickering flames and playful maracas. Get out the new game directions and let your imagination go crazy.

"Recipe for Romance" Essentials

Follow this recipe to the T or whip up your own creation by adding or substituting goodies.

1 Twister game
2 sets maracas that light up
1 large sombrero
1 Latin music CD
2 margarita glasses
3-5 colorful votives
3-5 mosaic votive holders
1 bottle massage oil
1 box hot tamales
1 margarita wooden block stamp and ink pad
new naughty rules (download at www.SexyandSparkling.com)

Mix It Up

This lively escapade screams fun! From the moment you start rounding up your romance essentials (most found online) to the time you and your man get twisted, you'll be feeling young, sexy and alive. Design an exciting presentation by laying the maracas, CD, Twister board spinner and hot tamales on the rim of the sombrero with the invitation strategically placed. (Depending on how and where you deliver this, you can add a bottle of tequila and the margarita glasses to the rim of the sombrero for effect.) Get out your Twister mat, read the new naughty rules, and use your margarita stamp as suggested. Practice so you know which moves are most alluring!

Passport to Passion Invitation

Pique his curiosity with these delivery options:

- Deliver to his office.
- Put on the front seat of his car.
- Let your imagination run wild!

How to Set the Mood for Romance

- Lighting: put colorful votive candles in mosaic holders and place around the room
- Music: *The Best Latin Party Album in the World* CD
- Location: den
- Tease: playful maracas

Get Your Sparkle On!

- Wardrobe ideas:

For you: flattering fitted top that's comfortable to move in and a sarong skirt (or long scarf wrapped as a sarong), bare feet with pretty, bright painted toes

For him: sombrero, shorts and tank or t-shirt—something comfortable

- Persona: Sassy Señorita

- Attitude: playful, adventurous, hot

Feed His Passion...and Yours

Share bite-size appetizers and tease as you feed each other setting a flirty tone for the evening. (Recipes found at www.SexyandSparkling.com.)

- Beverage: Hypnotiq Margaritas—if alcohol is not your thing a virgin drink works just as well!
- Appetizers: "Deconstructed Nachos"—Baja guacamole, pico de gallo, tillas mias

How to Prepare for Your Romantic Adventure

Two weeks in advance:

- Order/shop or search your closet for your ensemble.
- If you're a mom, schedule a babysitter for the night of your adventure or, better yet, arrange for your kids to stay with family or friends.

One week in advance:

- Get your props and romance essentials together.

Day before:

- Prepare invitation.
- Prepare outfit.
- Shop for food.

Day of Romance-Capade:

- Deliver invitation.
- Prepare appetizers.
- Set up props.

Cold Feet?

Even though you want more romance, stretching to make that happen can make you feel a little anxious—perfectly normal. Take a moment to remember why you wanted to create this fun and passionate adventure in the first place. Being brave enough to do something different will take your relationship to a new level, build your confidence and make you feel vibrant and alive. Set yourself up for success with a support system. Here are a few suggestions:

- Ask a girlfriend to be on standby for a pep talk or an encouraging text.
- Pump yourself with positive self-talk.
- Dance to your favorite music.
- Do a meditation/visualization.
- Do yoga to center yourself and limber up before he arrives!

You Can Do It!

Crank up the Latin vibe by shaking your colorful glowing maracas and unleashing your sassy side. Turn up the music, grab your lover and start a conga line threading your way through the house and ending up on the Twister mat. With the new racy rules you and your man will be screaming olé in no time!

* * *

Celebrate

Way to go señorita! Whether your Romance-Capade was a hit or had some unexpected twists and turns, congratulate yourself. Acknowledge your courage to muster your moxie and let your feminine playful spirit shine, bringing fresh new sparks to your relationship. Treat yourself to a glass of champagne with a friend, a long walk in nature, a decadent dessert, a massage, a bouquet of your favorite flowers. It doesn't matter what you do, it only matters that you do *something* to celebrate YOU.

What's Next?

Now that your sparkling mojo is soaring, get out your planner, set a date for your next Romance-Capade and keep the momentum going. Do it now, before life gets in the way. If you put it on the back burner you're not only being stingy with yourself by not living into your full creative expression, you're cheating your relationship too. Remember love has four letters, GIVE. So gift yourself and your love life with another fun-loving adventure.

Meet Me at the Kasbah

🔥🔥

Step into Moroccan romance by transforming your den with earthy pillows, candlelight and a feast fit for a king. Slip into a sexy belly-dancing costume before greeting your love at the door with a Morocco Mary cocktail and some sensual shimmy shaking. Invite him into the palace den for an exotic ride on your magic carpet, three juicy wishes and a mesmerizing dance of the seven veils. Sizzling!

"Recipe for Romance" Essentials

Follow this recipe to the T or whip up your own creation by adding or substituting goodies.

1 belly dancer or genie ensemble
music
3 Moroccan candle holders
2-4 Moroccan tea lights
3 richly colored pillows
1 magic carpet
1 Aladdin's lamp

Mix It Up

Get your girlfriends to take a belly-dancing class with you and make some fun memories while connecting with your feminine in a very powerful way. Learn how to do the dance of the seven veils as a strip dance by watching Rita Hayworth's YouTube clip. Study the looks and moves she makes to captivate the king—literally taking his breath away. (Head's up: the ending is a bit bizarre!) Let your vivacious vixen out!

Passport to Passion Invitation

Pique his curiosity with these delivery options:

- Put it in an Aladdin's lamp and drop by or send to his office.
- Attach it to belly dance clicker and put it in his jacket pocket.

- Let your imagination run wild!

How to Set the Mood for Romance

- Lighting: dim, lots of candle light
- Music: Moroccan
- Location: den
- Tease: dance of the seven veils

Get Your Sparkle On!

- Wardrobe ideas: belly dancer or genie outfit (find online or in a costume shop)
- Persona: mysterious, exotic
- Attitude: seductive, flirty, pleasing

Feed His Passion...and Yours

Sensually feed each other the suggested nibbles below. Sharing these bite-size appetizers in an intimate way sets the tone for the evening. (Recipes found at www.SexyandSparkling.com.)

- Beverage: Morocco Mary—if alcohol is not your thing a virgin drink is just as good!

- Appetizers: Casablanca spiced lamb skewers with tabbouleh, pita, feta & artesian olives

How to Prepare for Your Romantic Adventure

Two weeks in advance:

- Order/shop or search your closet for your ensemble.
- If you're a mom, schedule a babysitter for the night of your adventure or, better yet, arrange for your kids to stay with family or friends.

One week in advance:

- Get your props and romance essentials together.

Day before:

- Prepare invitation.
- Prepare outfit.
- Shop for food.

Day of Romance-Capade:

- Deliver invitation.
- Prepare appetizers.
- Set up props.

Cold Feet?

Breaking out of your comfy cocoon can cause you to get anxious—that's normal. Bolster your bravery with a support system that gives you courage. Then, choose to put your big girl panties on and go for the gusto! Here are a few suggestions to help you quiet the screaming meemies:

- Ask one of your girlfriends to be on standby for support or an encouraging text.
- Give yourself a mental pep talk.
- Dance to your favorite music.
- Do yoga or other centering exercise.
- Do a meditation/visualization just before he arrives.

You Can Do It!

As you prepare for this sexy adventure think of the exotic and mysterious attitude of a belly dancer—she's one of your leading ladies that wants to come out and play! Breathe her into your mind, body and spirit. Embrace this essence! As you move through the evening, falling into oversized pillows, feeding each other exotic finger foods, dancing the seven veils, and granting wishes as his private genie, call upon her to give you the courage and creativity to step outside your comfort zone and create a night of unforgettable passion.

* * *

Celebrate

You rock! Whether your adventure went off without a hitch or took an unexpected turn, kudos to you! You were bold and daring and had the courage to express your feminine fabulosity and add sizzle to your relationship. Treat yourself to a glass of wine with a friend, a sexy new frock, a decadent dessert, a massage—whatever makes you feel honored, special and celebrated!

What's Next?

To help your relationship stay passionately alive, select another saucy adventure and get it on your calendar. Do it now! With your busy life months will fly by in the blink of an eye so flip through the following pages and decide what you want to surprise your partner with next. Keep the momentum strong!

Let's Burn It Up!

Ignite the flames of passion by creating an inferno of love. Set the mood with alluring red light bulbs and slip into your sexy velvet panties. Feel your senses sizzle with desire as you sensually massage each other in front of a roaring fire...Burn baby, burn!

"Recipe for Romance" Essentials

Follow this recipe to the T or whip up your own creation by adding or substituting goodies.

1 fire hat
1 "fire extinguisher" (a can of whipped cream wrapped in red paper)
2 red light bulbs
1 pair black lace or velvet panties
1 "Light My Fire" sheet music
1 *Light My Fire* Doors CD (or your desired music)
1 small bottle of massage oil
1 tin of cinnamon Altoids
1 package black raffia
1 package red foil tinsel
1 large cellophane gift bag
1 Let's Burn it Up invitation

Place black raffia and red foil tinsel in the bottom of the fire helmet and arrange all other romance essentials on top. Wrap it all up in a cellophane bag and send it off.

Mix It Up

Make this a fun adventure from start to finish by grabbing one of your gal pals and heading to the nearest fire station. Practice your flirting and tell the guys on duty about the fiery escapade you're planning. Trust me, these hunky heroes will be totally intrigued and jumping

to help you. See if they've got an old fire hat—the relics are the best. Not only will you and your girlfriend have a ball, but what a story to tell your sisterhood!

Passport to Passion Invitation

Pique your man's passion with this hot invitation in one of the following ways:

- Send it to his office.
- Leave it on his car seat for a morning surprise.
- Let your imagination run wild!

How to Set the Mood for Romance

- Lighting: fireplace on and/or red candles and/or red light bulbs in place of those boring white ones
- Music: "Light My Fire"
- Location: living room
- Tease: Scatter red and orange rose petals to create a trail to you. Leave a note on the outside of the door to the house: "Follow the path of rose petals to your fiery damsel in distress..."

Get Your Sparkle On!

- Wardrobe ideas: soft and feminine, flowing dress and pretty shoe
- Persona: damsel in distress
- Attitude: vulnerable and grateful

Feed His Passion...and Yours

Sensually feed each other the suggested nibbles below. Sharing these items together in an intimate way sets the steamy tone for the evening. (Recipes found at www.SexyandSparkling.com.)

- Beverage: Pepe's Flame of Love Martini or non-alcoholic Orange Cocktail
- Appetizers: "Love Me Tender" peppered filet mignon canapé with horseradish crème, Blackened Scallops with Smokin' Hot Chorizo Cream Sauce, Baby Bellas stuffed Crimini mushrooms

How to Prepare for Your Romantic Adventure

Two weeks in advance:

- Order/shop or search your closet for your ensemble.
- If you're a mom, schedule a babysitter for the night of your adventure or, better yet, arrange for your kids to stay with family or friends.

One week in advance:

- Get your props and romance essentials together.

Day before:

- Prepare invitation.
- Prepare outfit.
- Shop for food.

Day of Romance-Capade:

- Deliver invitation.
- Prepare appetizers.
- Set up props.

Cold Feet?

Even if you deeply desire a more passionate relationship, trying something new can be a bit scary. Have a support system in place to help you get your courage up and calm your nerves. This may be set up in a variety of ways but make sure you plan for it so you don't chicken out! Here are a few suggestions to help you own your sexy Self:

- Ask one of your girlfriends to be on standby for support.
- Give yourself a positive pep talk.
- Breathe in deeply and let out a loud, pleasured "Haaaaa."
- Exercise.
- Do a meditation/visualization just before he arrives.

You Can Do It!

Visualize yourself having the time of your life: you're slow dancing to sultry music, sipping martinis as you feed each other sensually, connecting emotionally and physically, tempting and teasing. Soft and sensual, you are ever so grateful that your big strong fireman is there to rescue you!

* * *

Celebrate

Way to go, wild and wonderful woman! Whatever the outcome of your romantic escapade, honor yourself for taking action. That might mean uncorking a bottle of champagne and toasting your fun-filled spirit with your fabulous friends (possibly inspiring them to indulge *their* inner vixen) or treating yourself to a massage or sending yourself a special congratulatory card—it doesn't matter what you do, just do *something* to celebrate YOU.

What's Next?

Now that you've got your relationship nice and toasty keep the embers burning by planning your next Romance-Capade. Get out your calendar, pick a date, and circle it in red. Do it now! If you put it on the back burner months will fly by and the flame will flicker out. To keep your relationship passionate flip through the pages, choose another hot adventure, and watch your love explode!

The Love Lounge

*Create a sultry and sexy scene (work that boa!) that "stirs and shakes" the senses. Smoky red lights and soulful music will set the mood for your evening of passion. Take center stage as you play the part of a lusty lounge singer (*à la *Eartha Kitt) with a voice as smooth as honey and a smoldering gaze to match. Feel your new persona peak as you pull on your red satin gloves. Add a playful tickling feather to your act and welcome your man to the Love Lounge!*

"Recipe for Romance" Essentials

Follow this recipe to the T or whip up your own creation by adding or substituting goodies.

- 1 oversized martini glass
- 1 white boa
- 1 pair of red satin gloves (elbow length)
- 1 red tickling feather
- 2 red light bulbs
- 1 matchbook with cinnamon incense matches
- 1 heart shaped red candle
- 1 cigarette holder (12″)

Mix It Up

Imagine you're mixing a cocktail that's the most sensual concoction ever! You are the star ingredient (enchanting element), of course, but all the playful goodies in your oversized martini glass add to your glamour and divadom. The brush of your boa, the tickling feather, the satin gloves…all will entice and excite his senses and mesmerize his eyes. The smell of cinnamon, one of the top aphrodisiacs, will stimulate his desire—use it liberally and with confidence. You're in good company—the Queen of Sheba used this scent to captivate King Solomon!

Passport to Passion Invitation

Invite your man to this provocative show in one of the following ways:

- Send the martini glass full of goodies with invitation attached special delivery to his office.
- Leave a singing message on his phone: "Hey Big Spender, come spend a little time with me...I can show you a good time at the Love Lounge..." Give the address and show time and sign off "Your Singing Siren, don't be late...."
- Let your imagination run wild!

How to Set the Mood for Romance

- Lighting: switch out white light bulbs with smoky red ones, light some candles
- Music: Peggy Lee's "Fever" or make your own compilation of lounge music downloaded to a CD
- Location: den
- Tease: boa

Get Your Sparkle On!

- Wardrobe ideas: red wig, long sequined dress (black or red) with thigh-high slit, red gloves, rhinestone necklace and bracelet, sexy stiletto or pretty low-heeled shoe. Shop at second-hand stores or go online to eBay or a costume site.

- Persona: lounge singer/diva
- Attitude: sultry and seductive

Feed His Passion…and Yours

Flirt and feed each other the suggested finger foods below. (Recipes found at www.SexyandSparkling.com.)

- Beverage: Lovely Hips—rosehip laced litchi martini & candied ginger matchsticks. For non-alcoholic substitute club soda for vodka.
- Appetizers: "Casual Comforts" Thai toasted cashews & rosemary-parmesan steak frites, filet mignon with shroom ragout and roasted garlic cream cheese mashers

How to Prepare for Your Romantic Adventure

Two weeks in advance:

- Order/shop or search your closet for your ensemble.
- If you're a mom, schedule a babysitter for the night of your adventure or, better yet, arrange for your kids to stay with family or friends.

One week in advance:

- Get your props and romance essentials together.

Day before:

- Prepare invitation.
- Prepare outfit.
- Shop for food.

Day of Romance-Capade:

- Deliver invitation.
- Prepare appetizers.
- Set up props.

Cold Feet?

Turn your fears and doubts into inspiration by watching the *Fabulous*

Baker Boys and study Michelle Pfeiffer's character. Look at legendary lounge singers like Diana Krall and Anita O'Day on YouTube. In addition, it's smart to have a support system in place.

- Ask one of your girlfriends to be on standby for encouragement.
- Say the word "yes" repeatedly as well as the phrase "I can do this."
- Use body movement/dance to connect with your sensuality.
- Do yoga or other centering exercise.
- Do a guided meditation/visualization just before he arrives.

You Can Do It!

Once you've chosen an artist to emulate, practice owning her songs. If you are blessed with a beautiful voice, tantalize your man with your own sensual sounds. Before your big night, practice in front of a mirror or get a friend involved to help you hone your act. Play with different moves and try on various facial expressions—everything from a smoldering gaze to a knowing smile to a wicked wink. Welcome your man to your love lounge. As you begin to purr like a kitten let your femininity flow. Grab your boa and do a sensual slide under your backside or trail it behind you, or wrap it around your man. Unleash your inner diva!

* * *

Celebrate

Kudos for being bold, daring and courageous enough to step outside your comfort zone! Credit yourself for expressing your feminine playful spirit and adding sizzle to your relationship. You are FANTABULOUS! Journal your experience. How did it make you feel? What worked well? What would you do differently next time? Make sure you celebrate!

What's Next?

Now that you've stepped into your stilettos keep them on! By all means switch them out, but don't take them off. Give all your sexy personas a chance to shine by immediately picking another Romance-Capade. Pick a date! Mark your calendar! Start planning!

Paris at Dawn

🔥🔥🔥

Start the day diving into delicious by creating a breakfast to remember for you and your amour. As his bodacious barista you'll be serving him the "Sunrise Special" full of tasty treats and sizzling surprises.

"Recipe for Romance" Essentials

Follow this recipe to the T or whip up your own creation by adding or substituting goodies.

1 transparent apron or silky bathrobe or birthday suit
1 pair maribous
1 tiara
1 breakfast tray
edible undies for you and your man (optional)

Mix It Up

Whether you wear a see-through apron, flowing silky bathrobe or nothing at all, choose the level of daring that feels right. It's most important that you feel comfortable so you are free to let your sensual side surface. Ask a friend to help you shop for the perfect kitten-heeled maribou. Try it on in different colors and see what shade matches the mood you want to create. Add the tiara (found online or at a bridal store) for glamour and attitude. Bonus option: if you're feeling full of va-va-voom and you want to throw in a special surprise, get yourself some edible undies (online)—for him too!

Passport to Passion Invitation

Pique his curiosity with these delivery options:

- Before he retires turn down the bed and place invite on his pillow with a chocolate.
- In the morning wake him up with a text invite.
- Let your imagination run wild!

Rendez-vous café au lait?

Steamy? Flavored? Whipped Cream?

How to Set the Mood for Romance

- Lighting: natural sunlight streaming through the window
- Music: French, "April in Paris"
- Location: bedroom
- Tease: transparent apron or lacy bathrobe

Get Your Sparkle On!

- Wardrobe ideas: a transparent apron or lacy bathrobe, kitten-heeled maribou and a glittering tiara are all you need
- Persona: Susie Sunshine
- Attitude: energized, happy and flirty

Feed His Passion…and Yours

Use your body as a plate for him to feast upon. No utensils allowed! (Recipes found at www.SexyandSparkling.com.)

- Beverage: mimosas—if alcohol is not your thing orange juice straight up works just as well!
- Appetizers: berries, whipped cream, "Angel Toast" amaretto battered angel food cake with toasted almonds, sausage links

How to Prepare for Your Romantic Adventure

Two weeks in advance:

- Order/shop or search your closet for your ensemble.
- If you're a mom, schedule a babysitter for the night of your adventure or, better yet, arrange for your kids to stay with family or friends.

One week in advance:

- Get your props and romance essentials together.

Day before:

- Prepare invitation.
- Prepare outfit.
- Shop for food.

Day of Romance-Capade:

- Deliver invitation.
- Prepare appetizers.
- Set up props.

Cold Feet?

Having second thoughts? We all become a bundle of nerves when stretching our limits. Trust that your personal and relationship growth are well worth a little anxiety. Here are a few suggestions to help you calm down and work your *ooh la la!*

- Ask one of your girlfriends to be on standby for support.
- Say the word "yes" repeatedly as well as the phrase "I can do this."
- Blast Edith Piaf's *"Non, Je Ne Regrette Rien"* ("I Regret Nothing")
- Breathe in deeply and let out a loud, pleasured "Haaaaa."
- See yourself smiling and happy afterward.

You Can Do It!

You are in glittering company…did you know Elizabeth Taylor wowed Mike Todd wearing nothing but a tiara and stilettos while making breakfast? Why not follow her lead? Remember, you are the BEST most bodacious barista in Paris—own it! Show off those hot little maribous letting them dangle deliciously off your foot. Add a light, flirty mood combined with a service-oriented attitude—he's going to feel like the luckiest man alive. Starting your day with a yummy rendezvous will move you right out of romantic rut into rock solid love.

* * *

Celebrate!

You did it! *Magnifique!* Give yourself a big hug and honor yourself for taking action. Whether everything went according to plan or you had to swing into Plan B acknowledge your brave and beautiful spirit. That might mean letting out a whopping wooohooo, dancing to your favorite song, calling and sharing your adventure with a friend or treating yourself to your favorite flowers—it doesn't matter what you do, just do *something* to celebrate YOU!

What's Next?

Take the time now, while you're feeling very French and fabulous to flip through the pages and choose your next Romance-Capade. What coy kitten wants to come out to play next time? Get excited! Not only are you freeing the different facets of your personality, you're kindling romance, passion and depth in your relationship. Pick a date for your next romp and start creating!

Pirate's Booty

🔥🔥🔥

Send your lover on an adventurous treasure hunt to find YOU! Whether you lead him to a restaurant, a hotel or the back seat of your car, it will be one frisky frolic when he claims his pirate's booty. Ahoy!

"Recipe for Romance" Essentials

Follow this recipe to the T or whip up your own creation by adding or substituting goodies.

1 clear glass bottle
1 Treasure Map (download at www.SexyandSparkling.com)
2-3 strands colorful Mardi Gras beads
1 eye patch
1 bag of gold coins
1 pirate booty bag (pillowcase or burlap sack)
1 compass
1 perfumed panty
2-5 lanterns
music

Mix It Up

Every man loves a treasure hunt! Invite a girlfriend to get involved and help you mastermind this fun adventure. You'll have a blast creating clues, thinking of treasures for him to find and coming up with sexy suggestions to write on your gold coins. Once you've designed your swashbuckling course mark your map, burn its edges and place in a glass bottle with colorful beads and seashells (all can be found at a craft store). Put it with the booty bag he'll use to collect the treasures (i.e., compass, eye patch, perfumed panty, drinking glasses) you've hidden along the way. Text your love and let him know where to find his treasure map, building his anticipation for this intriguing escapade. Yo ho!

Ahoy **My Sexy Mate!**

Shiver me timbers,
a booty of bliss is at stake...

xoxo...Pirate Princess
P.S. Your Treasure Map awaits...

Romance-Capades™ ***www.SexyandSparkling.com***

Passport to Passion Invitation

Pique his curiosity with these delivery options:

- Roll up invite with rope and an eye patch—place in his glove compartment. Start the fun with a text, "Check your glove box... for a sexy adventure."
- Scan and email with subject title, "Tonight! Intriguing treasure hunt! Are you in Captain Jack?"
- Let your imagination run wild!

How to Set the Mood for Romance

- Lighting: lanterns and low lighting
- Music: soundtrack from *Pirates of the Caribbean*
- Location: your home
- Tease: treasure map and pirate booty bag

Get Your Sparkle On!

- Wardrobe ideas: shop at a costume store or online for a sexy pirate outfit
- Persona: Pirate Princess
- Attitude: hard to get, feisty—lots of pirates want you!

Feed His Passion...and Yours

Create intimacy and excitement by sensually feeding each other these nibbles. (Recipes found at www.SexyandSparkling.com.)

- Beverage: Cuba Libre or non-alcoholic "Thai Me Up" organic tangerine juice with Thai basil simple syrup
- Appetizers: Jerked Pork Carnitas with Caramelized Plantain Hash Hash

How to Prepare for Your Romantic Adventure

Two weeks in advance:

- Order/shop or search your closet for your ensemble.
- If you're a mom, schedule a babysitter for the night of your adventure or arrange for your kids to stay with family or friends.

One week in advance:

- Get your romance essentials together.
- Decide on the treasures to be found.
- Mark your map with treasure locations ultimately leading to YOU!
- Write acts of love on the gold coins—massage, juicy kiss, foot rub, etc.

Day before:

- Put treasure map in bottle with beads.
- Prepare outfit.
- Shop for food.

Day of Romance-Capade:

- Deliver invitation.
- Place your treasures according to treasure map.
- Set out your bottle with map and booty bag.
- Prepare appetizers.

Cold Feet?

Lost your sea legs? Having second thoughts? It's normal to feel a bit nervous any time you stretch your comfort zone. Trust that your personal and relationship growth is well worth any jitters. Here are a few suggestions to help you calm your nerves before stepping into your saucy adventure:

- Ask one of your soul sisters to be on standby for support.
- Give yourself a dose of positive self-talk.
- Dance to your favorite music.
- Do yoga or other centering exercise.
- Do a guided meditation/visualization just before he arrives.

You Can Do It!

Embody the essence of being the "Pirate Princess." Delight in the mystery and intrigue your hunt has created for your guy and imagine the fun you will have when he's finally found you, the most coveted treasure of all. Increase the value of the booty by playing a game with your bag of suggestively marked gold coins. Scatter them across the floor and give him 20 seconds to collect as many as he can. Put them in a treasure chest and with eyes closed let him choose up to three for the evening. After that he can claim one coin per week to return to the pleasures of a pirate's life.

* * *

Celebrate

Bravo, Pirate Princess! Take the time to enjoy the spoils of your daring and courageous spirit. Acknowledge and honor the action you took to bring fun romantic adventure to your relationship. Celebrate by having lunch with your posse of girlfriends and brag on yourself—you may just inspire them to explore their buried passions. Buy yourself a pretty pair of panties or a yummy smelling essential oil to continue the "feel good." It doesn't matter what you do, it only matters that you celebrate YOU!

What's Next?

Now that you've got your mojo flowing, get out your calendar, set a date for your next Romance-Capade and keep the momentum going. Do it now! With your busy life weeks will turn into months without an encore unless you have a plan in place. If you want a passionate relationship, commit to pleasure and playtime and pick another adventure!

Mystery & Mischief

🔥🔥🔥

Meet your beau at a hotel bar and act as though you are strangers. Send him a drink with a note saying, "I saw you on the subway this morning and have to have you…meet me at room #…get ready for a wild night of passion."

"Recipe for Romance" Essentials

Follow this recipe to the T or whip up your own creation by adding or substituting goodies.

1 Femme Fatale ensemble
1 hotel room and key
1 small velvet pouch

Mix It Up

To prepare for this steamy adventure ask one of your fabulous friends to help you check out the bars in local hotels. You'll want something on the dark side, kind of loungey and retro feeling. Your girlfriend can also let you know which location offers the best lighting. Get the bartender on board with your sexy plan—believe me, he'll be all over it! You'll need a room so plan for an overnight stay. As for your luscious lingerie...go bold and daring!

Passport to Passion Invitation

Pique his curiosity with these delivery options:

- Put it in his pocket as he's leaving the house.
- Put it in his briefcase.
- Let your imagination run wild!

How to Set the Mood for Romance

- Lighting: choose a bar with low, flattering lighting
- Music: piano in the background if possible
- Location: bar of choice
- Tease: trench coat

Get Your Sparkle On!

- Costume: trench coat with nothing underneath but lacy lingerie and a garter belt, sexy pumps or boots. For a wild card wear a wig.
- Persona: Femme Fatale
- Attitude: mysterious, alluring

Feed His Passion...and Yours

Eat with pleasure driving him wild!

- Beverage: Golden Dawn Martini or virgin drink of your choice
- Appetizers: natural aphrodisiacs on the menu—oysters, shrimp, sushi, asparagus, nuts

How to Prepare for Your Romantic Adventure

Two weeks in advance:

- Order/shop or search your closet for your ensemble.
- If you're a mom, schedule a babysitter for the night of your adventure or, better yet, arrange for your kids to stay with family or friends.

One week in advance:

- Get your props and romance essentials together.

- Check out hotels with bars.

Day before:

- Prepare invitation.
- Prepare outfit.

Day of Romance-Capade:

- Deliver invitation.
- Prepare velvet pouch with key and note.

Cold Feet?

Nervous? That's normal—any time you step outside your comfort zone you're going to get the jitters. Take a deep breath and remember why you wanted to create this mischievous adventure in the first place. Your bravery will take your relationship to a new level, build your confidence and make you feel vibrant and alive. Put some backup support in place to help you calm your nerves:

- Ask one of your girlfriends to be on standby for support.
- Say the word "yes" repeatedly as well as the phrase "I can do this."
- Exercise.
- List the positives this escapade will provide you personally as well as your relationship.
- Do a meditation/visualization before you meet with your man.

You Can Do It!

See yourself as a mysterious woman, very "film noir." You may want to watch some old movies from the '30s and study the leading ladies to get the persona down. When your big night arrives, meet your lover at the bar as though you're strangers, and coyly reveal your lingerie over drinks. Excuse yourself and have the bartender give your guy a naughty note asking him to meet you upstairs in your hotel room. Of course you're waiting…without the trench coat…

* * *

Celebrate

Wooohooo! You are AMAZING! Give yourself a big hug and make

sure to acknowledge and honor the action you took to bring romantic adventure to your relationship. Celebrate by having lunch with your circle of friends and brag on yourself—you just may inspire them to unleash their inner desires. Buy yourself that high calorie latte you love but never allow yourself to have or a sparkling piece of jewelry or send yourself a special card of recognition. Celebrate YOU!

What's Next?

Now that your *vavoom* has surfaced with such sensation, keep it in the spotlight by immediately choosing another Romance-Capade. What dazzling diva wants to come out to play next? Get to know all of you and you'll be thrilled to see how your creative expression illuminates you from the inside out AND keeps your relationship revved up and sparkling. Pick a date! Mark your calendar! Start planning!

Romance-Capade #15

Playboy Mansion

🔥🔥🔥

Send your sweetheart a camera with an enticing note letting him know he's won a once-in-a-lifetime opportunity to photograph a Playmate (you, of course!) in some luscious lingerie and strappy stilettos. Best of all, he gets to call the shots!

"Recipe for Romance" Essentials

Follow this recipe to the T or whip up your own creation by adding or substituting goodies.

camera
music
candles
risqué lingerie
Playboy bunny outfit

Mix It Up

You may want to bring your friends in on this red-hot rendezvous for some sexy masterminding. They can help you hone your steamy poses, plan your props, pick out your Playmate accessories and shop for outrageous lingerie. Even if you've got it all figured out on your own involving your posse makes it more fun and gives you added support.

Passport to Passion Invitation

Pique his curiosity by delivering the invite with a camera in the following ways:

- Hide it in his underwear drawer the night before with the bunny ears for a morning surprise.
- Put in a bag marked "Playboy Mansion Winner" and place within his radar in the morning.
- Let your imagination run wild!

How to Set the Mood for Romance

- Lighting: favorable
- Music: *9½ Weeks* soundtrack, Ann Margaret's "Let Me Entertain You"
- Location: living room, patio if private and weather permits, hotel room
- Tease: Playboy bunny ears

Get Your Sparkle On!

- Wardrobe ideas: Playboy bunny teddy and accessories: headband, collar with bow, cuffs, tail (order online). Have other risqué lingerie ready for wardrobe changes: short nighty, corset and garter with stockings, baby doll. If you're feeling adventurous work it with a wig! Strappy stilettos.
- Persona: confident, outgoing, "I'm all that," fearless
- Attitude: sassy, sizzling

Feed His Passion...and Yours

Whet his appetite with these suggested nibbles. (Recipes found at www.SexyandSparkling.com.)

- Beverage: Manhattan with a maraschino cherry or non-alcoholic Honey Bunny
- Appetizers: fresh veggies and dip, Truffled Macaroni–n-Cheese, G.C.Me petite grilled cheese squares with tomato-basil dipping sauce

How to Prepare for Your Romantic Adventure

Two weeks in advance:

- Order/shop for your lingerie and bunny outfit.
- If you're a mom, schedule a babysitter for the night of your adventure or, better yet, arrange for your kids to stay with family or friends.

One week in advance:

- Get your props and romance essentials together.

Day before:

- Prepare invitation.
- Prepare outfit.
- Shop for food.

Day of Romance-Capade:

- Deliver invitation.
- Prepare appetizers.
- Set up props.

Cold Feet?

Feeling like you wanna chicken out? Any time you stretch your comfort zone it's natural to feel a bit anxious. Have faith that your bold action will change the dynamics of your relationship for the better. Muster your moxie with a support system that gives you courage. Here are a few suggestions to help you calm your nerves before you set the lens on fire!

- Ask a supportive friend to be on standby to give you a last-minute pep talk.
- Say the word "yes" repeatedly for inner strength.
- Exercise.

- Do a guided visualization just before he arrives.
- Breathe in deeply and let out a loud, pleasured "Haaaaa."

You Can Do It!

Start this fiery photo shoot with a sexy walk down a stairwell, if you have one, or let him find you lying seductively on a lounge chair. Have a tray with drinks and appetizers waiting and a passionate movie (*à la 9 ½ weeks*) playing that would capture the attention of Mr. Hefner himself. Explore different backdrops, throw a furry blanket on the bed, and let your hot sensual poses burn up the lens. *SSSSSSTTTT.*

* * *

Celebrate

Huge kudos for being brave, daring and courageous enough to step outside your comfort zone! Credit yourself for expressing your feminine playful spirit and bringing some mega watt sparkle to your relationship. You are PHENOMENAL! Journal your experience—how it made you feel, what worked well, and what you'd do differently next time. Celebrate with LOTS of pampering!

What's Next?

Now that you've busted out of boring keep your relationship fresh and exciting by picking another Romance-Capade pronto! Keep those stilettos on and stepping out! Get to know all of you by giving your cast of sexy personas permission to surface and shine. You'll be thrilled to see how your creative expression not only brings back your sparkle, but keeps your relationship radiant as well. Pick a date. Mark your calendar. Start planning. Get going!

Resources

The people we encounter, the articles and books we read, the movies and television programs we watch, and the events we attend all influence us on a daily basis.

Although I haven't kept a journal of all the great works I've been privileged to learn from, the following resources stand out as the most inspirational, enlightening and motivational in my journey to complete this book. This list does not represent everything or everyone I've benefited from, nor does it signify the vast knowledge out there available to you, but it is a good, strong start.

Books and Articles

The Abundance Book by John Randolph Price, Hay House, Inc., 2005

"The Benefits of Human Touch" by Carmen Jochmann, Health Field @ suite 101, October 15, 2009 http://carmen-jochmann.suite101.com/the-benefits-of-human-touch-a155979

"The Benefits of Laughter" by Hara Estroff Marano, Psychology Today, April 29, 2011

The Biology of Belief: Unleashing the Power of Consciousness, Matter, & Miracles by Bruce H. Lipton, Hay House, Inc., 2011

A Complaint Free World: How to Stop Complaining and Start Enjoying the Life You Always Wanted by Will Bowen, Doubleday, 2007

Eat Pray Love by Elizabeth Gilbert, Penguin Books Ltd., 2006

The Four Agreements by Don Miguel Ruiz, Amber-Allen Publishing, 1997

"How Laughter Therapy Improves Skin Tone" by 3 fat chicks on a diet! http://www.3fatchicks.com/how-laughter-therapy-improves-skin-tone/

Images of Desire by Jaqueline Lapa Sussman, Tom Doherty Associates, 2001

"The Imposture Syndrome" by Satoshi Kanazawa, Psychology Today, July 26, 2009 http://www.psychologytoday.com/em/31314

In the Meantime: Finding Yourself and the Love You Want by Iyanla Vanzant, Simon & Schuster, 1999

Jesus Calling: Enjoying Peace in His Presence by Sarah Young, Thomas Nelson, 2004

Louder Than Words: Nonverbal Communication by Mele Koneya, Alton Barbour, Merrill, 1976

Mama Gena's School of Womanly Arts by Regena Thomashauer, Simon & Schuster, 2002

The Mastery of Love by Don Miguel Ruiz, Amber-Allen Publishing, 1999

Meditations for Manifesting: Morning and Evening Meditations to Literally Create Your Heart's Desire by Dr. Wayne Dyer, Hay House Audio Books, 1995

"Positive Thinking: Reduce Stress by Eliminating Negative Self-Talk" by Mayo Clinic staff, Mayo Clinic, May 28, 2011

http://www.mayoclinic.com/health/positive-thinking/SR00009

Sacred Contracts: Awakening Your Divine Potential by Caroline Myss, Sounds True, Inc., 2001

"Science Confirms That Women Reap Health Benefits from Friendship" by Melissa Healy, The Seattle Times, June 15, 2005 http://seattletimes.nwsource.com/html/health/2002335724_healthwomenfriends15.html

The Soulmate Secret: Manifest the Love of Your Life with the Law of Attraction by Arielle Ford, Harper Collins, 2009

Spiritual Growth: Being Your Higher Self by Sanaya Roman, HJ Kramer, 1989

The Success Principles by Jack Canfield, Harper Collins, 2005

"25 Ways to Become a Legendary Flirt" by Korin Miller, Cosmopolitan http://www.cosmopolitan.com/sex-love/dating-advice/become-a-legendary-flirt

"What Are Friends For? A Longer Life" by Tara Parker-Pope, The New York Times, April 20, 2009 http://www.nytimes.com/2009/04/21/health/21well.html

You Can Heal Your Life by Louise L. Hay, Hay House, Inc., 1987

"Your Soul Needs Playtime" by Emma Seppala, Spirituality & Health, May/June 2011

Movies

Baghdad Cafe, directed by Percy Adlon, 1987

Dangerous Beauty, directed by Marshall Herskovitz, 1998

The Holiday, directed by Nancy Meyers, 2006

It's Complicated, directed by Nancy Meyers, 2009

Last Holiday, directed by Wayne Wang, 2006

Secretariat, directed by Randall Wallace, 2010

Sex and the City, directed by Michael Patrick King, 2008

Sex and the City 2, directed by Michael Patrick King, 2010

Something's Gotta Give, directed by Nancy Meyers, 2003

Workshops, Interviews and Services

Dr. Michael Bernard Beckwith, Agape International Spiritual Center

Ti Caine, Future Visioning Expert, interviewed by author 2010. www.TiCaine.com

Jack Canfield and Jim Bunch, The Ultimate Life Workshop, 2008

Patty Contenta, interviewed by author, 2009

Ellie Drake, Meet & Greet, 2011

Tarnie Fulloon, interviewed by author, 2008

HRock Church, 2011

Karen Johnson, PSYCH-K Advanced Workshop, 2008

Chef Brian James Lucas – www.ChefBeLive.com

Linda Penny, Chakra Sound Tuning Fork Therapy Workshop, 2009

Dr. David Schnarch, interviewed on Today, 2006

Sophia Sharpe, interviewed by author, 2009

Katherine Woodward Thomas and Claire Zammit, Feminine Power Telecourse for Awakening Women, 2010

Chef Scott Wagner – www.ChefScotty.com

About the Author

Sherri Nickols is an award-winning author, motivational speaker, women's empowerment coach and Sparkling Mojo Specialist. She is a highly trained expert in helping women balance their masculine and feminine energies as well as overcome the negative patterns that keep them stuck. With her transformational tools, her business, Unleash Your Inner Sparkle, teaches women how to connect with their natural feminine power. Through her work as a coach and educator over the past decade, Sherri's signature "playshops," romance parties, teleseminars, articles, and private coaching have helped thousands of women around the world open their hearts to create healthy, loving relationships, reconnect with their sensuality, rediscover their joy and bring romantic adventure into their lives.

Sherri specializes in making transformation fun—helping others get unstuck so they can unleash their beauty and brilliance, attain inner peace, love with freedom and leap into a bright future. She loves clients who are motivated to make lasting change.

Sherri is a certified advanced PSYCH-K facilitator and holds certification in Tuning Fork Sound Therapy and Transformational Healing. A lively talk show guest, she has appeared on "CBS KCAL9," "Good Morning San Diego," "View From the Bay" and "San Diego Living." The author lives in Los Angeles, California.

To learn more about Sherri's "playshops," teleseminars and coaching:

www.UnleashYourInnerSparkle.com

www.SexyandSparkling.com

To connect with Sherri:

Twitter www.twitter.com/sherrinickols

LinkedIn www.linkedin.com/ pub/sherri-nickols/9/1b9/913

Facebook www.facebook.com/snickols1

YouTube www.youtube.com/user/snickols1

To read her articles:

www.YourTango.com

www.ArticlesBySherri.com

Sherri Nickols offers a variety of services and products to help women get unstuck and move into a bright future. Whether single, married or divorced you'll learn how to design a fun and joyful life and create the soul-to-soul connections you desire. You can participate in one of the programs below, give yourself the gift of private coaching, or both!

Telecourses

5 Weeks to Discover & Own Your Playful, Sexy Self! This five-week teleclass is for those who want to break out of a romantic rut and learn the secrets to a love life full of romance and passion. http://www.RelationshipSparkle.com

The SPARKLE System™: This eight-week telecourse will deepen your understanding of the SPARKLE System. The course gives you a more personalized experience that enables you to successfully integrate the tools and strategies. Laser coaching on the calls will also give you the opportunity for individualized attention. After this course you will feel more fully alive, living with vibrant joy

CD's

Get Your Sparkle On! These three 30-minute guided visualizations will help you increase confidence, connect with sensuality and open your heart. "Sparkle with Confidence," "Sparkle with Sensuality," "Sparkle with Love." http://www.SexyandSparkling.com

Sparkle with Feminine Power: This 30-minute guided meditation uses tuning fork sound therapy to open your feminine heart center, balance your energy and improve your connection to your sensuality. http://www.SexyandSparkling.com

Coaching Progams

Sparkling Mojo 12-Carat coaching package: A fun way to transform your life, this package offers four one-on-one private coaching sessions dedicated to creating your brilliant future and helping you get unstuck. http://www.UnleashYourInnerSparkle.com

Sparkling Mojo 18-Carat coaching package: Make lasting change with this private coaching package of 10 one-on-one individual sessions. We'll start with designing your ideal future and then focus on successfully overcoming the negative thoughts and behavioral patterns that keep you from stepping into that beautiful life. Includes *Get Your Sparkle On!* – these three CD's will help you embrace change more easily. http://UnleashYourInnerSparkle.com

Sparkling Mojo 24-Carat coaching package: If you are ready to unearth your magnificence this 90-day private coaching program is for you! Includes 15 one-on-one sessions, tuning fork therapy, *5 Weeks to Discover & Own Your Playful, Sexy Self!* Telecourse, three essential oils chosen for your specific needs, *Get Your Sparkle On!* Kit, *Sparkle with Feminine Power* CD and nine expert interviews to help you rev up your radiance. Beginning with a guided visualization specific to your dreams you will see and feel what is possible for your life. Together we will uncover and heal your limiting beliefs, then create actionable steps resulting in 180-degree changes. You will be given the tools to successfully overcome depression, sadness, betrayal, disconnection and disempowerment while increasing self-esteem and confidence. Free from fears that have kept you stuck you will live with passion, trust and joy – excited about your life! http://www.UnleashYourInnerSparkle.com

Romance-Capade ™ Hot Line: Do you want to step into your stilettos and give voice to your creative expression? This one-on-one private coaching session will help you plan your very own, unique romantic rendezvous. http://www.SexyandSparkling.com

Sexy and Sparkling Workshops: Fun and interactive live events designed to awaken your feminine essence and sensuality. In a very safe haven, with the support of a small group of women, you'll be able to break out of your patterns and learn how to become the sparkling woman you were born to be!

Sexy and Sparkling Retreats: Inspirational, experiential fun adventures in spectacular settings. These one-of-a-kind retreats will open your mind and heart to a new way of being, allowing you to step with ease and enthusiasm into your sparkling essence.

About Sherri Nickols Coaching

Call or email Sherri today to schedule a complimentary 30 minute no obligation coaching session.

(818) 923-5102 info@SexyandSparkling.com

Share Your Story

So...how did it go? Whether you rocked it or had a few twists and turns, please share your Romance-Capade adventures with me at http://www.SexyandSparkling.com.

I'll be reading each one personally and would love to know how it made you feel, what it did for your relationship, how you celebrated and what's next! What worked? What would you do differently next time? Did you use one of the escapades in this book or create one all your own?

Your feedback will be vital to my next book—a collection of even more sizzling Romance-Capades—so step into your magnificence and share, share, share!

To your Sexy, Sparkling Self!

QR Code

To access the book website scan this code into your smart phone.